good deed rain

Books by Allen Frost

Ohio Trio
Bowl of Water
Another Life
Home Recordings
The Mermaid Translation
The Selected Correspondence of Kenneth Patchen
The Wonderful Stupid Man
Saint Lemonade
Playground
Roosevelt
5 Novels
The Sylvan Moore Show
Town in a Cloud
A Flutter of Birds Passing Through Heaven:
    A Tribute to Robert Sund
At the Edge of America
Lake Erie Submarine
The Book of Ticks
I Can Only Imagine
The Orphanage of Abandoned Teenagers
Different Planet
Go with the Flow: A Tribute to Clyde Sanborn
Homeless Sutra
The Lake Walker
A Hundred Dreams Ago
Almost Animals
The Robotic Age
Kennedy
Fable
Elbows & Knees: Essays & Plays
The Last Paper Stars
Walt Amherst is Awake
When You Smile You Let in Light
Pinocchio in America
Florida
Blue Anthem Wailing
The Welfare Office
Island Air
Imaginary Someone

IMAGINARY SOMEONE

Imaginary Someone © 2020
Allen Frost, Good Deed Rain
Bellingham, Washington
ISBN: 978-1-64633-560-2

Writing, Drawings: Allen Frost
Author Photo: Rustle Frost
Cover Production: Jen Armitage
Apple: TFK!

Some of this writing also appears in:
Bowl of Water, Another Life, Home Recordings, Playground, The Sylvan Moore Show, Town in a Cloud, The Peaceful Island, When You Smile You Let in Light, Florida, Violet of the Silent Movies.

Heard melodies are sweet; but those unheard
       Are sweeter

   —John Keats

IMAGINARY SOMEONE

Allen Frost

Good Deed Rain ◊ Bellingham, Washington ◊ 2020

It is then that he slips into another world altogether, a world where his imagination takes over and he finds himself actually living *in the places he is writing about*

—Roald Dahl from "Lucky Break"

This book takes place from 1967 to 2012—forty five years in the life of an imaginary someone.

CONTENTS

A Mountain Stream Memory
A Long Time Ago in California
A Movie Cupped in the Hands
My Rocket School
Good Morning
1972
A Girl
The Ghost Town
Mockingbird Clock
Garage Theater
Night Flight
Very Far Away
August 16, 1975
The Blue House
The Count
Japan
Allowances
Shortcut
North 48th Street
Carried Along By the Wind
The Klickitat
Friday Harbor
Trees

How Come?
The $5 Ghost
The Flight to Mars
Blue Eyes
Clock Radio
What Sad Flowers
Astronomy
Typing Class
Twice the Sun
My First Date
Rememory
Me & Mars
Origami Brother
Dowsing
A Nautical Memory
On the Road to the Ocean
More than One Blue Moon
The Story Just Happened Like the Radio On
Fred Again
How to Open a Coconut
Asleep on a Steamship
In New Orleans
Radio
The Dummy Family
Bicycles
A Frog and A Pig
Dandelions
3 Ghosts
A Couple Hundred Years Ago
Life is a Movie Always Waiting to Come True
The Day the Earth Stood Still

The Jellyfish Movie
Dolphin Trainer
Perfect Chance
Why Models Stand the Way They Do
The Green Chairs
The Brooklyn Deer
Castle in the Desert
A Famous Author
A 20 Year Old Movie
Mourning
What's Wrong? I Heard Voices
A Letter from 1990
A Bargain with Emily Dickinson
Dante's Grill
The History of Motown
Her Comfort Disappeared in Green Smoke
Miles To Go Before We Sleep
It Could Only Be Loud, With Electricity, in the Dark
Cube
Shrug
September 4, 1991
The Dragonfly
Rabbit
The Little Black Cat
The Curse Trance
Gasworks
Gasworks Stars
Good Day Tea
Chocolate
Walls Could Be Walked Through
The Television Bodhisattva

Royalty Toy Company
December 11, 1992
The Princess of Sadness
April 18, 1994
June 10, 1994
Her Spells
The Old Goat
Clinton Street
Filming Caruso
Still Creek
In the Steam
The Love Nest
Back to Memory
A Baby
The Greyhound
The $50 Rabbit
This is Who
Ohio Tornado
The Kaleidoscope Cat
The Opening Act
A Garage in Ohio
The 1940s
State Farm
The ½ Creature
A Factory Job
The Bicycle Tomb
Slow Leak
Franklin Lilacs
River Stones
On a Wet Corner
King Medicine

September 24, 2010
A Living by Writing
The Journal of The Mermaid Translation, part 1
The Journal of The Mermaid Translation, part 2
The Journal of The Mermaid Translation, part 3
Ohio Silver Mine
The Bicycle Chronicles
The 5 Year Old Land
Walking with a Flower
One Raining Night
North Cascades
The Poetry Phenomenon

A MOUNTAIN STREAM MEMORY

One year old
watching water
turned gold
by the sun

A LONG TIME AGO in CALIFORNIA

I've been told the story so I guess it happened this way.
A long time ago in California, we went to Disneyland.
My Uncle Mike tagged along quietly. He was still a
teenager in school when he flew out from Maine.
I guess I made a fool of myself, crying over a turtle
and was still crying as we left the kingdom,
into the wide parking lot, looking for our car.
Before we could find it, or even realized
Uncle Mike was gone, he reappeared like magic,
running over the hot tar with that puppet
on the end of his hand.

A MOVIE CUPPED in the HANDS

Leaving the sun and ocean world, looking out
the back crescent window of a Volkswagen beetle
waving to the people I would never see again.
I still see them standing there. Waving to two
waving girls—the taller seems to be wearing
a reddish burgundy dress perhaps, but she had
dark curly hair, thick. Holding the other's hand
maybe, but disappearing slowly. Arriving in Seattle
nighttime green, it was a different planet.
The place we stayed in had a huge, tall tiger
in the hallway. Orange, white, stripes and teeth.
Later, the first grade at my school, during lunch
they let us watch the rocket going to the moon.
People got excited about things like that
it's an almost inconceivable America
compared to the one we're in today
(with its wars and doom wall of fears)
though I also remember my father
making sure I watched Nixon impeached.
We spent a lot of time running the neighborhood
after school, our whole block was a Treasure Island
map with a secret alley, shortcuts through yards
the best trees to climb, my favorite one the laurel
with soft green almost fur on its bark skin
I would climb up to the top and hold on.
I could see blue sky through the leaves,
sometimes airplanes. Spent a lot of time
in the Imaginary. Friends were always found
who made this most alive. Below the branches

in my friend's yard, we would snap little twigs
to make the miniature houses of a whole town
set among the weeds. The bugs would be
the people walking back and forth.
At school the best time was making books,
drawing, recess, the library and those rare times
when the lights would be dimmed, the clacking
curtains came down and a movie projector
was rolled to the back of the room.
I can never forget the sound of that
magic machine with the film running through,
from drum to drum, making a bright beam of
light in the air where some story came to life
on the rolled down screen over the blackboard.
Reaching a hand up into that movie river.
When it was done, before the movie got shut
in a round metal can, we always had to beg
the teacher to let us see it backwards and
sometimes we got to. What could be funnier
than people running in reverse, impossible
actions and surprises, the story you knew
going back to where it began.

MY ROCKET SCHOOL

Memories in the elementary yellow room, I could trade a banana with Luis for a matchbox car, where chasing tag games would end in a fight and Tyrone could slap a kid so hard he'd have to get stitches, where across the street from the school was that strange white tiered apartment building holding the half-vampire, half-werewolf man kids would go see on a dare—stories of him transforming and they'd run back down the stairs over to school before he could kill you, where on the school bus kids would show off SST dragsters, talk about the gorilla at the museum. Remember walking into a classroom, the smell of chalk dust nearby, under the American flag, boy, girl, boy, girl, to return to our silver legged desks. There was a girl who drew round headed people with button noses that I thought was an artistic breakthrough and copied for a while, where on the wall paper plate face self portraits of all the kids in our room in colored rows. Coming in early from paper bag lunch break to watch rockets take off from Florida, land on the Moon, where I brought my sister in once for show and tell, and where I was astounded by the fact that numbers could go backwards from zero, into another dimension. And then there was the riot. My fingers clung to the mesh wire chain link fence to watch through to the other side, down the tarred slope to that big broad pavement plateau where there are fire truck hoses shooting on protestors, streams of water, and riot gear cops with plastic shield and visors. Screams and rocks flying, tear gas drifting.

And us children watching from up above with only a fence between us and them.

GOOD MORNING

A crow left the blue gray sky
spun like a leaf and landed on
the peaked roof of a green house.
Below was a window. A light glowed
on the glass, making it a golden square.
It was a school day, I had to be up early.
There were dinosaurs on the floor,
railroad tracks and airplanes, an open
book by Dr. Seuss. The blankets were
dragged half off the bed, I had
already gone downstairs.
I was eating cereal, King Vitamin,
and watching a show on TV. Black and
white waves flowed from the screen.
A clown who lived in the city dump
would spin a ragged dartboard target
nailed to the door of his shack and a
cartoon would magically appear.
Cats dancing on a wooden fence,
a rocket ship, a haunted house
strung like prayers all part of
the morning path to third grade.

1972

In third grade we got divided up for the election. I remember we had a chant, "McGovern, McGovern, he's our man! Nixon belongs in the garbage can!" We drummed and stomped and sang around. With our red white and blue streamers and flags, the yellow light in the room seemed to get brighter.

A GIRL

A girl went missing in our neighborhood.
Posters of her were put up on telephone poles.
They lined the sidewalks. I remember
the photo of her in a white dress
long dark hair.

The GHOST TOWN

Our van broke down in Montana or the Dakotas
and we were marooned in one of those little towns
with tall flat brick walls. The painted messages
were fading off like ghosts. We did a lot of that
walking around, exploring. We tied our dog
in front of a diner while we ate. Afterwards
we walked on down the street until our dog
just froze. She became a statue, set in cement.
With her head down, she wouldn't take a step
further. There was some invisible barrier
she had run into. We weren't stopped though,
we could move far enough from her to read
the writing on the glass window of the store.
Taxidermist. In the gloom, I could see
a whole cemetery of animals, frozen by chemicals
and wires into man-made imitations of life.
The only way past all those glass eyes
was to pull our dog across the street
out of their sight.

MOCKINGBIRD CLOCK

We had the choice of sleeping on the floor in the room with the cuckoo clock, or we could set up the old army cot on the porch. There was also an old metal porch swing. Of course that was always the preferred choice. In the early break of dawn, I would wake up to hear the mockingbird, the sunlight spreading across the cow field.

GARAGE THEATER

It was a garage. The big fold-down door was up so you could see inside. There was a curtain in the middle with the old forgotten things pushed to either side and a few rows of chairs set up, leading right out to sidewalk. The summer nights were nicest, the warm air, the trees filled with paper lanterns, most of the neighborhood turned out to watch. The newspaper even had a story. In September, when school started again, the plays happened less frequently. Sometimes you would see a bright pen drawing stapled to a telephone pole. You would go that night, even if it meant standing on the curb, under the drumming umbrellas where the rain was part of the play.

NIGHT FLIGHT

I dreamed of stepping out on that place where the green roof tiles sloped and flattened enough for a perch, just outside my parents' window, stretching my arms and flying. And at blue night, with lights sprinkled twinkling whites and orange beyond the park and lake, clouds low, purple flocks, it almost seemed possible.

VERY FAR AWAY

My bedroom with that BB pellet hole in the window where my mother had been framed in its midnoon gold glass in front of me, shielding, and then she opened the window too and yelled out loud for whoever took the shot to stop. It was probably some kid testing out his new birthday gun and meaning no more harm than a movie star. "This is a house! A house isn't a target for guns!" Afterwards, I could put my finger over that small cratered impression and feel the tiny pulse of outside cold. Just a memory faded away like the colors of cloth, like the pale yellow surfboard that was gaining inches of dust in that nook under the stairs, where spiders dwelled and you wouldn't dare put your hand there without the aid of a flashlight. The same cellar where my father and I started to build a fort out of balsa wood dowels after seeing one in a museum. But we got no further than one wall before the board it was on became the base for a grander vision—a railroad set that Christmas brought in a Sears box wrapped up in bright colors that reflected the glow of that happy morning when, "OK…Go!" on our parents' urge, we raced down the carpeted stairs in our pajamas. Those were the stairs I fell down so many times in the months it took to master them and the stairs which became such a feature in my dreams that they still reappear to this day—stairs that you can either fly down or they descend down, down into dark, and it's hard to turn around and come back up. Entering that Christmas morning world of happy screams, the dog is barking from the kitchen behind the barricade where I had drawn crayon on the wood, 'Help Me!' with a picture of a spider in a web, but the dog was barking Christmas excitement too as we leaped about in the circle of tree lights and presents and our parents came down the stairs after us and smiled. Happiness was as simple then as making up mysterious adventures for driving a Big Wheel, cruising the block, the plastic back tire click-clicking the faster I drove on my mission, loud just like a real motorcycle. I drove around the cement block passing all the houses and ivy covered walls and there were dogs that would bark, birds that would fly out of the way, cats that would slink across my path or sit in the shade of porches. And back behind houses I would race urgently, quietly trespassing with friends, imaginary enemies chasing us and stories unfolding as we went or, "Watch out!" the worst thing of all—dinosaurs crunching fences and trees and roaring across the city skyline. Great beasts beat the air, hot on the trail for kids who ran away and tried to hide. Or sometimes things got real small, building little houses in the dirt, with leaves for roofs and twig walls, miniature architecture for rock people or little animal toys from cereal boxes. Other animals came from those revolving trays wheeled in the display case at the toy store, where horses, cows, anteaters, hippos, bears, pigs and dogs and ducks would be revealed under your eyes as you pressed the button to see the waterfall of animals move. You pick one and the old guy behind the counter would hear you say, "A-7," and he'd pull out the little green box with the clear plastic front where you could see the white horse and the knight on its back. On the way home you would play with your present on the back of the seat, making the horse trot on the black rubber edge, investigate the ashtray which was only used for depositing Juicy Fruit or Blackjack gum, close it with a click, and move on exploring…There were no beginnings or endings then, just a period of time that stands out now like a still-living reality and I remember once at the dentist being asked about braces (the same dentist who afterwards would let you pick a prize from the trunk in the back room—a green soldier made in Hong Kong, or a silver airplane, or if you were lucky, a dinosaur). He told about the way of teeth, that one day I should think about getting braces, but I didn't have to worry about it until I was twelve. 12. Of all things, my favorite number! But I remember being glad, that was a long time away, thinking to myself, "That's good. I'll let him worry about that when the time comes." *Him*, another me, seeing then my life as stages, where that will be a different person in the future. And I probably still think that way, time, those times, *him*, I remember you and you are very far away.

AUGUST 16, 1975

Our next door neighbor came to our door
with her hand wrapped in a red towel.
It was Elvis Presley's death that sent her.
She was in grieving and tried to cheer up
with a big slice of chocolate cake.
Sadly, it was in the freezer, hard as a brick
and the knife sliced her instead.
My father drove her to the hospital.
I didn't know much about Elvis then.
I liked his song "In the Ghetto."
Advertised as part of a record set
it appeared during commercial breaks
in my Saturday afternoon monster movies.
That weekend she took my sister and me
to the circus. Before we got to the big tent
she pointed her bandaged hand skyward.
High above the parking lot, a man ran
inside a cage, tiny as a white dot
with everyone on the ground watching
waiting for him to fall.

The BLUE HOUSE

Go over the fence or through the gate to the neighbor's yard under the laundry line and past the big climbing tree beneath the green leaves and shade past where the weeds grow wild around the little dirt town with miniature house built for the bugs. My friend's house is on the corner. The cement wall drops down to the sidewalk where I sat talking about Jack and the Beanstalk that led to some games in the tree then we went inside. Sometimes I bring a sleeping bag in my arms so we can watch the monster movies at midnight. We filled the basement with a cardboard box maze. Once we were running upstairs and I took a splinter through my toe. I went to the hospital for that. And once we were throwing rocks and I broke a window. Their house made the loudest noise and froze us all like photographs.

The COUNT

A long time ago in a different America Friday night
meant staying up late to watch The Count.
Transmitted to our black and white TV at 11:45 PM,
his *Nightmare Theatre* would feature the weirdest
stories of monsters, islands with foggy cobblestones
and castles. Sometimes I would go to my friend's,
carrying my sleeping bag, through two backyards
under washlines and trees. It was a long wait
as the windows went black until finally,
by then in sleeping bags, The Count's show began.
Wolves howled, thunder, a ghoulish organ wheezed,
and the camera would ease you at a slow walking pace
past the stone dungeon walls, a burning torch, towards
his waiting coffin. The Count was very real to us,
I don't think I ever doubted him, he lived to haunt us.
One Halloween, my father made a cardboard coffin
for our porch. Dressed as The Count, he terrified
trick-or-treaters. I could hear them shrieking
far up the nighttime street from our house.
Probably that same Halloween the real Count
was appearing at the Seattle Center.
At blackest night of course. I remember him
on the spotlit stage in his cape. Green skin.
Behind him was the Haunted House, which
I refused to enter. He waved other people in,
but I could see the shaking cage with a gorilla
striking out furry arms. I knew all about gorillas
from watching his show. All The Count's movies
have turned into hovering dreams in me.

Of course movie hosts were a dying breed.
By the 1980s they were virtually extinct.
The last one I remember seeing in the Seattle area
was the *Dialing for Dollars* host (who survives
in one of my novels) and a guy named Red
who was only there to plug his restaurant
on Lake City Way, interrupting Bela Lugosi
like a waiter with a menu.

JAPAN

Just across the ocean a few thousand miles away
I knew Japan by what washed ashore here.
From the movies I watched, I found out about
their troubles with giant monsters, Godzilla,
Gamera, Mothra and Rodan. It seemed that
the people there couldn't go anywhere,
on water, or strolling through the woods
without a sudden attack. The creatures
especially loved to kick through their cities
like toys, setting them afire, then leaving
mysteriously. So I would watch for them
on Seattle's skyline. Over the baseball field
at night where the glowing arc lights turned
purple higher up, was something huge floating?
I could look out the window upstairs and see
the hill, the park trees and the zoo and dream
a dinosaur appearing. I would read in my room
Japanese folktales, the Peach Boy, dragons,
sea turtles and princess birds. When the sky
was blue there was a place on the avenue
half a block from the Food Giant grocery,
my favorite store, Fuji's Five and Dime,
painted black with white letters, fish flags,
down the aisle to the toys or the candy
surrounded by bright plastic gold and jade
tea sets and Buddhas of all sizes.
Going home, carrying bags,
watching over the tall telephone poles
holding electric wires up past the leaves,

Japan was in the clouds that floated
all the way over here.

ALLOWANCES

Fuji's Five & Dime store used to be in Wallingford on 45th Avenue. I'd go there with allowance coins and buy Blackjack gum or a box of rice candy, a rubber dinosaur, or a flying machine. Sometimes I'd let money fill up the elephant bank. Sooner or later I'd go to the 7-11. Down our block, across the street, there was a path through the community garden. Depending on the season, it could be tall sunflowers and rows of vegetables. Later it grew tar and turned into a parking lot.

SHORTCUT

A way
we know
goes between
concrete walls
narrows
in weeds
and shadows
Don't mind
the cobwebs
They grow
when we
aren't here
cutting through yards
climbing wooden fences
between the leaves
knowing the secret
saving time
like summer sunlight
kept in a jar with
a raindrop

NORTH 48th STREET

After another day
climbing green trees
playing through yards
and down alleys
games that claim
the whole neighborhood
as the world
sitting on the steps
and listening

I'm remembering

As the sun sets
if the wind is right
on those summer nights
I can hear the zoo
transmitted on the air
like radio

A lion roars
calling out
from his throne
in a cage
diminishing in waves
like a stone
carried out
over the rooftops

CARRIED ALONG by the WIND

Getting to evening, magic in the air, blue dusk falling like hourglass sand. The sidewalk poured in squares making concrete cracks to hop over. A tan cat on a wooden fence watching, yellow eyes unblinking. Clouds are purple, pink and blue, swallows bee-ing low, the beginning crackle of firecrackers. The houses packed together close, sloping grass towards the sidewalk. An old woman walking a small brown dog with red collar. A harp in the window of a house with lessons to offer. Go carefully on the big street, 45th, don't cross until the red hand shows on the light. American flag from a wooden porch rail. Pop and snap of firecrackers, a shrieking firework sets dogs off barking. Two cats, black and white, on a green and brown patched lawn. Church of brick and stone, tower the tallest thing in the neighborhood. A light streak, a banging echo. Faded hopscotch squares sanded by the feet of kids. School light left on outside, shines a green white. A firework passes by like a bright dying kite and pops into nothing with a gunshot. Gunpowder smell. Sweet fragrance in the air too, from a flower branch hanging over the sidewalk. Stray black dog jangling his tags as he runs between parked cars, sniffing. Four Square painted in fresh yellow for girls in sweater skirts. That dog jingles away at a fast run. A bumbling of jangled bottles. A whistle and a boom. On to the next street, houses, all these ancient well known sights. Kids in trick-or-treat formation playing with sparklers. A man with a dropped red flare at the sidewalk watches his little girl dancing around, waving a flag on a stick. "Oh boy! Careful now, not too close." Thunder and fireworks. Past the house with a green and yellow tree. Music next door, playing and laughing. One man lets off a screeching, whizzing wild show that set the kids screaming and some lady howling, "Oh, that was real great!" Trees whisper. Further ahead, the triangle shaped storage building, brown like a slice of cake, it used to be canary yellow. Clouds just explode. There's Big Wheel Corner, a whoosh of three plastic wheels rumbles by me. Children left a shallow wading pool filled with cool water and toys. A bat and a bicycle, overturned on the lawn. A pinwheel beating in the warm wind. An American flag clinging below to a cold cellar wall seen through a green lit window. A block away, the ghost of the neighborhood garden long since mashed into a parking lot. Tall flowers, weeds, grown in small places, colors bloom the July sky.

The KLICKITAT

Up on the deck of the Klickitat,
what a perfect name for a ferryboat,
clacking all over with every lean
it makes, or change in the current
sending a shiver down the keel
turning in the green water
between the tall rocky islands.
Made of planks bolted in
like lily pads, all the rust
heavily painted over
evergreen and white.

FRIDAY HARBOR

I've been coming to this spot
for most of my life, a rock on top of the hill
overlooking a harbor full of green water

TREES

That big Seattle climbing tree next door really created friendships with all its footholds, roosts and views offered. Up I'd climb, believing myself a koala or bird, I'm sure. Whatever game we wanted to play the tree would adapt. When we moved out to the forest and lived in the trees that got me seeing our world as one big connected rainforest being chopped down. I love to look out my rectangular night window and see the black shadow silhouettes of trees sway against the blue night sky with its stars humming bright.

HOW COME?

I wasn't on television for very long
I was on a program called *How Come?*
Making a giant pair of inflatable sunglasses
A few seconds worth of film for the day
They may have been hoping for more
A shot of the boy levitating dramatically
Riding the sunglasses out of the room
And into the air for a slow dissolving
Pan of him disappearing into sky

The $5 GHOST

My sister bought a ghost for five dollars.
Her friend arranged the sale and gave us
specific directions which we followed precisely.
First we wrote a welcoming letter to the ghost.
At 8 o'clock we opened the front door an inch
and placed the note beside a candle. We sat
in the hallway for a while, lit by the yellow glow.
We were tuned to the ghost frequency, listening
for the smallest sigh or voice, jumping at flickers.
I guess we were expecting a ghost to arrive with
a suitcase. I know I was. It was easy to believe
in that. But after waiting a while, my sister gave up
grabbed the letter and stormed to the phone.
Maybe we were swindled. It's hard to tell
when you're buying something invisible
and just because you don't see what
you expected, does that mean something
didn't happen? Who knows?
I shut the door, blew out the candle
and carried the smoke with me.

The FLIGHT to MARS

I think it's probably fair to tell
what's been evened out by time.
In grade school I won the award
and traveled by bus into Seattle
to the university to hear about
the wonders of being a writer.
But I didn't forget that boy who lost,
whose story was not judged best,
who wrote a science fiction about
another planet, a rocket, a monster
or something I don't remember.
I only know he carried a grudge,
enough to move across the room
and from then on to put on a cloud
whenever he saw me.
I felt bad about the way
it turned out, to think it was
a contest, his story versus mine.
All these years have grown to now
and I wonder what strange world
writing has taken him to.
All this time later I wonder
was he right about robots,
the loneliness of outer space
traveling out into the beyond.
Was it where he wanted to go?

BLUE EYES

In the 7th grade, she told me she saw the Loch Ness Monster. Her family skidded the car to a stop as the mysterious creature walked across the road in front of them. It was big as an elephant but it slipped like a shadow through the branches down into the water. I could believe it. The water got calm. She said she never told anyone and who wouldn't believe those blue eyes?

CLOCK RADIO

It sat beside my bed like a white cat.
I spent a lot of nights listening to baseball
especially tuning for the games from far away,
a strong signal, usually a California station
that would float in near like a moth flapping
around, sooner or later buzzing into static.
And then there were the shows: *Inner Sanctum*
or *Mystery Theatre*, detectives creeping
after murder. There was a timer on the side.
I set it so I could listen to my programs
while I fell asleep. On the weekend KVI
would play Jack Benny, Phil Harris,
Our Miss Brooks and other comedies.
I would hold a tape recorder to the speaker
like some castaway, as those radio waves
reached for me far in the future.

WHAT SAD FLOWERS

I was in a sunny kitchen
beside Lake Washington
when I read Bing Crosby died.
The newspaper was left
on the cluttered table
under sky blue flowers.

ASTRONOMY

The only time he phoned her
it was a comedy nightmare.
Loving her wasn't meant to be
but that truth was never clear
like a song by The Clovers
until one day after school
when he spotted her sister.
She missed the bus.
He went over beside her
to offer her a ride.
His mother drove them.
By the time they got to her house
it was obvious. She was the one
he would climb a ladder for
and throw a rope around the moon.

TYPING CLASS

Studying
the machine
trying
to do
my best
it's easy
to be
distracted
by a girl

TWICE the SUN

The simplest thing happened walking to class. Looking back over my shoulder for a second, seeing her—blonde hair, straight and long, a light blue sweater—walking towards me. She's going to class too, to the same study hall actually. And I stopped, turned around to her and joined her for our short time together, talking, walking. But her smile when I stopped and joined her was more than the sun.

MY FIRST DATE

I stood there
with flowers

yellow

REMEMORY

Before I really knew much about poverty
how it is used for terror and survival of the fittest
I remember her. Such long brown hair beauty.
She had moved from somewhere on the plains
to the green rain country. Her family grew Christmas
trees, tall sunflowers and corn; there were old cars
collapsed in front of her yellow house. Sometimes
I dream of her and the memory of her looks into me
when I sleep.

ME & MARS

For several months, I had a job making boxes, stapling cardboard into square shapes, stacking them into piles. I sat on a metal stool in front of the stapling machine, a Medieval thing, old and strange; it looked like an iron stork. By kicking a pedal at its base, it shot a staple into the cardboard which I folded and turned quickly like origami in its beak. A light bulb hung on a long black wire overhead and by the end of eight hours, the space around me would be surrounded by four walls of boxes. Near the end of the night and the beginning of morning, the night watchman made the rounds. Before he appeared, I could hear all those keys on his belt and the flashlight he carried would creep shadows ahead. His name was Mars. I have run into a Martian wall trying to remember him. My memory of Mars is so quiet, so far away, barely there, held together by strings. Everything about Mars seems to be covered with sand rust. I remember he was Ronald Reagan's number one fan. He would talk about war and the car he drove (something loose dragged underneath it and made dangerous red sparks on the ground).

ORIGAMI BROTHER

One day I was at her house, she made us
some instant coffee then left the kitchen
to get something. The cup was still too hot
to drink from. I watched the milk in it spin.
She returned from the little room carrying
a parchment. It didn't leave her hands
but she held it close enough for me to read.
I think an eagle was on it, above typed words.
Her brother Jimmy was killed in the war
by a Japanese kamikaze. She wanted me to see
that news unfolded like a paper airplane.

DOWSING

My grandfather was a dowser. Even though that sounds like the beginning of a short story it isn't because I never had time to learn that skill from him. I do remember walking in the wooded backyard while he looked for the right fallen stick. When he found one, he walked my cousin and I around until the stick moved in his hands. Pointing at the ground, he told us there was water there.

A NAUTICAL MEMORY

Floating about in a little Maine rowboat, it was really was no bigger than a bathtub. I used to go out deep and tip a look over to watch the big rocks, rooftops under there. I could see the world underwater, it was a mirror of up here, they had their little fish driving back and forth endlessly. Of course my grandfather would take us way offshore, stopping in those Atlantic swells, dropping handlines for codfish. Oy, those swells will get you sicker than a sea radish in no time, but not him. He was raised and lived on it, he could move on a wave.

ON the ROAD to the OCEAN

There was a boy keeping track of Russian history
(that was me) writing it all down on notebook paper
reading about the czars, the men and women,
the peasants who finally couldn't take it anymore.
Meanwhile he didn't know the slightest thing
about America. He worked at a gas station and
talked to a truck driver from Oregon one night.
Another man bought a lot of bottles, dropped them
in the parking lot, sliced his hand picking them up
and had to buy more. Still, it was nice when no one
was around and he could read, and the best part
of all was when he closed the store, counted receipts,
hid the money in the cooler and got to lock the door.
Outside, summer night blinking with stars and
meteors, he rode his bicycle home on the road to
the ocean.

MORE THAN ONE BLUE MOON

I used to listen faithfully to a radio station in Maine. On summer nights, it would play those old 1950s songs, doo-wop and R&B that I loved. One evening while The Everly Brothers were singing, or Fats Domino, or Mary Wells, I worked up my courage by the telephone. I remember the door was open to the porch and the ocean was out there. Across the bay, the little houses and vehicles were dots of reflected water light. It took me two more songs to pick up the receiver and dial. When the DJ answered, I could hear the music in the background like the soundtrack of a drive-in movie playing with mosquitoes in a chrome car-covered field. I asked if he could play "Blue Moon" and he said sure and hung up. That was all it took, but I felt instantly at ease again. I could breathe again. All I had to do was listen and wait for The Marcels. After a commercial break for the horse racetrack and Mammoth Mart, the DJ returned to the microphone and announced the next song was a special request and the needle touched the vinyl with a rushing crackle. Now, in those days, I did think of myself as one of those 1950s teenagers I saw in the movies, *Diner* and *American Graffiti*. I expected a lot from this DJ, you would have thought I was a moth caught in the glow of the radio dial. Except the song he played wasn't what I asked for, it was "Blue Moon of Kentucky" by Elvis Presley. Even though Elvis recorded "Blue Moon" in the echo chamber of Sun Studios, why didn't the DJ play that instead? Maybe he wanted me to know there was more than one blue moon.

The STORY JUST HAPPENED
LIKE the RADIO ON

Once with socks
on my hands
I lay below
an open window
for a puppet show
all I could see
was trees
the story
just happened
like the radio on
I didn't know
an audience
gathered
out there

FRED AGAIN

For a brief strange amount of time, I opened the doors to the Salvation Army and Goodwill to find my music. This is always a fallback into years of wear, from the clothes that hang and give the air its ghost, to the very back wall where the records are tipped stacks in a bin. I became familiar with the usual cast: Percy Faith, everything with strings, cowboys, swingers, preachers, patriots, dance crazes, and every once in while the true oddity. Something that had the power to stand up out of its pit of time and grab like a shaggy, ice-age creature. Something named "Whistlin' Joe," on a pink Decca Records label, by someone named Fred Lowery.

For 25 cents, the 45 single was given a whole new life, played over and over for days until its eerie warbling and spooky chorus became too much for one listener. He ran across the room, ripped it from the turntable and smashed it against the gray speckled wall. That fit, that terrible wax demise, seemed to have ended a life. Even my joy of searching the musty world where "Whistlin' Joe" once lay entombed passed. As a last wish, to serve eulogy to the person who had created such a stir in my life, I felt duty bound to know what I could about Fred Lowery. This was years before the computer captured the logging of all human details, and the only information on him I uncovered came from the few lines in a thick reference book: "Blind whistling virtuoso active in the late 30s and 40s. Attended Texas School for the Blind in Austin...

worked clubs and theatres; some recording. Faded by the late 40s; a few records early 50s."

I kept the intact pink round record label, the very center, the heart, all the remained of Fred Lowery's 45 and I have carried it forever as a sort of holy relic.

How strange that I would rediscover Fred Lowery some five years later at the other edge of the continent, in a retro-store dedicated to the hip and cool culture of America's past.

Filed in with the pristine Capitol recordings of Sinatra was an entire album by Fred Lowery entitled, *Walking Along Kicking The Leaves…* Surprise! He has risen again, wrapped in a Technicolor sleeve, whistling with orchestra, a bona-fide cult member of those who only seem to fade.

HOW to OPEN a COCONUT

Since you asked
my South Sea advice
this is the best way
to open a coconut:
start in the kitchen
push up the window
set it there
on the sill
and slam
the frame
down

Now
go out to
the parking lot
look around
find it rolled
under a car
bring it back
and try it
again

ASLEEP on a STEAMSHIP

Afternoon, a dark colored car going northbound
with the pines on either side of the highway
blurring by. While my friend drives, slumps
his face against the window, I crouch
on the floor out of sight with a hand on
the steering wheel, keeping us on course.
We were hoping that passing cars would
think he was asleep, though one eye was
barely open so he could direct me by degrees,
like one of those old steamships on a
pavement covered sea.

In NEW ORLEANS

When I was in New Orleans, we ended up in the room
of a famous Cajun cook. He was eighty years old.
We met him in a market and he invited us to his
apartment. There were faded *Playboy* centerfolds
on the wallpaper. He threw all of his groceries
onto a table by the window. "I'll be right back,"
he told us. "There's something I want to show you."
The door wasn't too far away, if we needed to
we could escape. In a minute, he returned, walking
like a pharaoh. He was carrying a clay planet shape.
"My son's remains are inside of this," he said.
Then he tripped on the warped floorboards.
The urn flew out of his hands in slow motion.

RADIO

We had a radio show in Maine that was unlike anything ever heard. There would be skipping records, a mayhem mix of sound effects, African horns and a drone from Tibet. On top of all that, Rob and I would make up convoluted dramas featuring detectives, bad jokes and time travel. This is where I first read a short story to a microphone. It was written on a shuffle of library catalog cards. We liked to think our show was leaving the Earth, the atmosphere and the galaxy on a long voyage forever. It was okay, somewhere out there a beautiful distant yodeling becomes a heavenly change of Victrola records, cowboys, mountain harmonies, jazz and minstrel words.

The DUMMY FAMILY

We created an entire family for only a few dollars
clothes, hats and shoes all bought at Goodwill
stuffed with newspapers, then placed in lying down
tragedy on the pavement of Maine Street at night.
They looked real enough to stop traffic and bring on
the roaring arrival of police with blue lights.
The family survived, carried home in a panic
over fences, across lawns in the dead of night.
We flopped them down on the apartment floor
and left them there. The Dummy Family was
a terrible failure, leading to our near arrest
so they spent a week thrown underfoot
like dead shadows beneath a pier.
Then one afternoon, I had a plan.
The father's fallen shape was just my size.
I took out his newspaper stuffing
and climbed into his Goodwill clothes.
I lay in his place on the floor and waited.
It was a terrible wait, I couldn't move,
I couldn't laugh and give it away as the door
finally rattled open. Dan came inside
and sat by a guitar. He started to play.
I watched through a little tear in newspaper.
I couldn't take it any longer. I leaped up
shouted, waved my arms at someone
I shocked into seeing a ghost.

BICYCLES

One night in college many moons ago, Scott and I raided the room where security would hide abandoned bicycles. The door was padlocked, but there was a gap above it and we could climb down inside. Bikes were piled on top of each other in there like ragged prisoners. They had given up hope ever seeing daylight again. We got as many as we could carry outside and stuck them in the trees over the campus walkway. The next day they were a source of wonder and the school paper even had a photo on the front page, baffled by who had done it and what it meant.

A FROG & A PIG

With college almost over, since a job was what all this learning was leading up to, the English Department announced a Career Day and brought in a publisher from New York City. Having written two novels already, I felt this was my chance. There were about ten of us in the wood paneled room, sun in the windows, it was warm outside. What did I know? I was reading Kerouac, I was ready to go. What the woman from the publishing metropolis offered was *The Muppet Babies* cartoon. She was scouting for writers. I couldn't do it, I couldn't even imagine it at the time, the squeaky voices, pastels and treacly jokes would have driven me mad. But now I wonder how hard it would be to twist my arm, to take me from my job and put me in a little blue sailboat with a frog and a pig and pay me to write the way out.

DANDELIONS

that door opened
to a morning
so golden with
the summer lawn
dandelions
overgrowing
tall enough
to wade through
like a sea
beside the sea

3 GHOSTS

The first ghost I recall was in my grandparents' house. I must have been seven or so. I woke up and saw it moving like a shadow across the wall. It got closer until I hid under the blankets. The next time was a few years later, at a house next to Lake Washington, the haunted room with its sewing machine and window painted shut, feeling the footsteps, staying awake, reading a paperback, listening with the light on until dawn. After college, a summer night in Maine, I was at a friend's house. I was asleep on the couch in the living room and I woke up with a white face only an inch from mine. I turned on the light quick and sat up until I couldn't stay awake anymore.

A COUPLE HUNDRED YEARS AGO

Our first failed Capitalist venture occurred one summer night when we went to the parking lot of the Shop N Save and tried to sell bright red t-shirts with smiling devil faces. Goat-headed, the evil one leered at the shoppers as they pushed their carts full of groceries back to cars. A couple hundred years ago they would have burned us at the stake, but now they ignored us and kept us trying to laugh, always on the edge of giving up.

LIFE is a MOVIE ALWAYS WAITING to COME TRUE

Like something I would do, my friend
fell in love with the deaf girl who bagged groceries
at Shop N Save. He kept trying to tell her in words
what she couldn't hear, and finally he decided to
write her a note. He bought some cheap cans
of chili and green beans and when she paused
to put them in paper, he passed her the letter.
Of course she was scared by what he spelled
the sudden words dropped out of the blue.
Who wouldn't be taken aback and need time
to figure out the mystery of you?
He had to go hide under the trees
the branches tied to the ceiling in his room
pale and sad with broken heart records hurting
when you take everything to heart and believe
life is a movie always waiting to come true.

The DAY the EARTH STOOD STILL

I remember the television
while the morning unfolded
out of night
while the stars turned
into daylight
The rest of the house
was asleep
The Day the Earth Stood Still
played quietly at dawn
flickering with a certain
black and white lesson

The JELLYFISH MOVIE

Walking along, we made up a movie, seeing it happen. The lights faded out like sunset, the curtains parted and onto the screen the flickering movie began. A father and son were fishing. Their feet dangled over the edge of the pier, the boy kicking his sneakers as the man sunk a hook through the worm and cast it out into sea. They talked about the baseball scores and laughed about their neighbor's car. Hungry gulls watched from the circling air and something else without eyes sensed them through the cold water. The boy tugged his fishing line, he thought he felt a bite. Small waves lapped around pilings and his father was telling him about the foot-binding tradition in Japan, when a weird noise bubbled towards them from the depth. It sounded something like a backwards foghorn being played in an oyster shell powered by rubber bands. A tense moment passed, then the father laughed, ruffled his kid's blond crewcut and lit a cigarette. His hands trembled, cupping the flame. Quickly, he threw the match into the sea. "When I was your age…" the man began to say, but suddenly the water turned into foam as a four-story jellyfish raised itself, gurgling out of the water and pulled them away. The water calmed down, the seagulls landed on the dock and ate their abandoned chicken sandwiches. That was it, the film slipping through the projector clacked at the end of the reel. The houselights came back on, calypso music played on speakers for the two people waiting for the next feature.

DOLPHIN TRAINER

After college, I decided I was a writer.
Unfortunately there is no defined path
to follow. I guessed it meant gathering
experience, reporting on the world.
Melville couldn't write about whales
until he had been to sea. So I began
with a long series of jobs, finding myself
filling out an application at a parking garage.
This would give me the perfect opportunity
to observe my world while spending time
reading and writing, maybe in a glass booth
bobbing about in a pond full of cars.
On the second page, I checked the box
for military experience, writing that I
was in the Coast Guard, filling the line
explaining it was a special program
teaching dolphins how to speak English.
Soon, I was called in for an interview
by a guy wearing an orange vest.
He could have been traveling in
the North Atlantic, but I was soon
to be wearing a vest just like it.
He didn't even ask me about my
Coast Guard experience.
The job paid minimum wage.
He brought me down the cement
staircase to the underground
parking lot. I had to march
up and down those aisles,

keeping account of spaces.
Cars were pulling in all the time.
After a while, I put a 'Parking Full'
sign out on the street level.
Then I could sit on my stool
where the wind blew in and read.
Sometimes the rain would lash down
or pour in rivulets past my chair
and it wasn't hard to think of those
cars as sleek creatures come searching
dipping beneath the waves.

PERFECT CHANCE

Suddenly I remember that house where I worked
stuffing envelopes with a nine year old. His father,
my boss, gave me the keys to his car one time so
I could pick it up from the garage. I took the bus
there to drive his rattling, barely repaired Chevrolet
back to work. On the way, I was overwhelmed with
a vision, the temptation to run it off the floating bridge
into Lake Washington...It was my perfect chance,
a wonderful thing I've seen in movies and always
wanted to do, crash a car off into sparkling water.
Minimum wage had delivered me this possibility.
Hopefully the cement barrier would burst like
plaster. Sinking, green water flooding in through
the vents and cracked glass, I would calmly take a
deep breath, roll the window down and swim up to
the surface where news crews and stopped traffic
would be waiting for my Hollywood emergence...
Unfortunately, I drove back to the job, parked his car,
went inside and got handed a rake. See what I could
do with the garden—there were weeds choking the
azaleas.

WHY MODELS STAND the WAY THEY DO

She was a model. You could tell by the way she stood at the filing cabinet. When I asked her why models stand the way they do, the unspoken attitude, the arms and body slant, she told me about Twinkies. They had changed their recipe, she said. She had been eating Twinkies for years, until recently when the sugar filling was changed. There was a loss in her voice as she talked about it in terms of the tragic crumbling of values. To her, this was the worst of America's crimes, and she decided to do something about it. She wrote them a letter that was burning her flag. She told them Twinkies had become uneatable. And she told me, even sadder, that she never even got a reply to her letter. It had now been over a year.

The GREEN CHAIRS

Someone left them on the street in Brooklyn
two chairs with glowing green upholstery.
Click that moment in your camera.
They looked like abandoned crowned jewels
on cold cement littered with broken glass.
Angels must have descended a subway in the clouds
bringing us this miraculous furniture.
It took Rob and I both to struggle them upstairs
tipping and turning them into our apartment
then letting them fall to the hardwood floor.
It was that impact that caused a thousand cockroaches
to race out of the thick cushions and springs
comfortably holding more than meets the eye.

The BROOKLYN DEER

Once upon a Brooklyn
we found a deer head
propped on the street.
Of course we carried it
down stairs into the station.
It was between trains
we climbed the wall and
stuck it in the rafters.
Glassy eyes watching
from the shadows
window lights flickering
the people come and go
from the city to the city.
It was a good hiding place
lasting there for several days
until someone spotted it
or maybe it took
the subway home.

CASTLE in the DESERT

When I lived in New York
I used to go to an old movie theater,
red as a velvet heart inside
with lamps on the walls.
I watched *My Little Chickadee*
with W.C. Fields and Mae West,
The Marx Brothers and Charlie Chan
finding the *Castle in the Desert*.
Homesick in one of the biggest
cities in the world.
I knew I was ready to leave
when it became my routine to visit
The Museum of Natural History.
Somewhere in all those displays
I would find the great wall of glass
holding a captured recreation of
the Pacific Northwest rain forest,
staring into the green light of
birdsongs, cedars and firs
in the middle of skyscrapers.

A FAMOUS AUTHOR

I remember that time I got the letter every writer waits for. I was walking with our dog, it was a sunny day, our path ran between yellow fields. I carried the big envelope about halfway, then stopped. I felt like Charlie Bucket with a Wonka chocolate as it slowly opened. My first novel had a note paperclipped to the manuscript. I read what they said and jumped in the air. The dog knew how I felt, she was a hopping black cloud around me. Then I read more. They liked it, but they wanted to make some changes. For $2000 they would edit although they couldn't guarantee its publication. I started to walk again. It was amazing how quickly I could be holding my novel, to holding a $2000 albatross. Fortunately, I didn't let that stop me. I had more books to write, even if it would take another ten years to have one published.

A 20 YEAR OLD MOVIE

I wonder where the statue ended up. I would have to contact some great detective—Sherlock Holmes or Charlie Chan—to pick up the trail made so cold by those long ago days. It started out as a block of clay my friend bought at a shop on Federal Street. It was a March afternoon, sunny with a cold wind. There was still some snow patched in every shadow. At home, it wouldn't take him long to work the clay, looking at a photo for reference, or pausing a favorite black and white video, frame by frame.

I feel I can still peer in through that window in Portland and see the statue he made. There...the size of a pineapple, at rest on the red formica table. There's a plant next to it. Maybe it's a cactus. When it was done, Buster Keaton lived in that kitchen. There was plenty going on around him. Stories, sorrows, music, laughing, all sorts of drama...it was like backstage in Vaudeville.

That's just one of those things I wonder about once in a while. It's a sort of legend, I guess, like a city of gold, a fountain of youth...the lost clay head of Buster Keaton. But what happened to it after my friend died? Clay has a better survival rate than people. Look at the ancient clatter in museums. It has the ability to outlive people by hundreds of years, so surely someone must have held onto that statue?

I'll admit there's not much to go on...a memory and wonderings. How could any mastermind track it down with only these clues? Maybe this is as close as I can ever get to it again...A picture in my mind like a photograph taken in a dream. There's Buster Keaton in some unknown location, watching a twenty year old movie go by in the blink of an eye.

MOURNING

It was morning, I was in bed, and his ghost tried to appear. A few days had passed since he had been taken out of water so it was on my mind that he was gone. Of course it troubled me more than you can know, all the phone calls he made before, and I didn't see where it was going and it took so much away. I rolled from the wall and looked at something forming in front of the bookshelf. The air was melting. I knew what was going to happen, but I couldn't watch. I looked away. I covered myself with blankets and waited for it to end. When I thought maybe it was safe, I looked back and nobody was there.

WHAT'S WRONG? I HEARD VOICES

"I believe that you loved him very much and that somehow you blame yourself for his death."
—*An American Werewolf in London* (1981)

I'm wondering about a movie I saw or maybe I just think I saw it. My memory of him is forever tied with movies. When I would take the bus into Portland to see him, we would talk all day and go to the public library where I'll never forget we got *The Day the Earth Stood Still* and *Invasion of the Body Snatchers* and we made up our own movies so real they might have happened.

A LETTER from 1990

The reason I'm sending you this small book is because it's an example of what I can do. All I want to do is write. I've written six books so far. When I was 19, I wrote the first one and sent it to Doubleday. They said, "your writing shows enormous talent and energy" but it wasn't publishable at that time. In the four years since then I feel like I'm really ready now, but I can't figure out this system of getting published. I'm not even sure exactly what the NWWG does. (I wish I could have sent this to Richard Brautigan but that's impossible). What I really need to find somehow is a grant that will allow me to distance myself from $5 an hour jobs for a while. It would be heaven to be able to just write and create books. How do I apply for a writing grant? Is it possible to hope for? I know this is the hope of everyone who writes but I've reached the breaking point, that's the only reason I'm asking. I just got laid off from my job and all my energy is being eaten looking for a cheap apartment and a new job. How great it would be to find a little relief from that. I am trying to self publish *Lawn Veterans*, a book of 25 stories about the cycle of life, but it's an uphill battle. Fortunately I've been discovering some real good inspiration lately. Like this: "Since the time of his youth, Crazy Horse had known that the world men lived in was only a shadow of the real world. To get into the real world, he had to dream."

A BARGAIN with EMILY DICKINSON

The sound of the typewriter keys late at night always revived Emily Dickinson's ghost. She arrived with chimes and a slightly cold wind that blew her into my room like a pillowy white smoke of rain. As always, she made me jump.

She rippled in the air.

I sighed a hundred pages piled around me. "I'm discouraged. I don't know what's going to happen to all of this," I admitted. "Maybe I'm only doomed to dream."

Emily stared at me, shimmering.

"And I have to get another job just to get by."

She laughed. Her ghostly hands swooped from her like birds.

"Easy for you to say." I wasn't in the best mood. The gloomy story I was writing was all about America as a Dr. Frankenstein creation and it was really getting to me.

She put her hand on my shoulder and whooshed it through my head in sympathy. "Don't worry," she said. "I'll help you. And you can do something for me in return."

"Sure," I agreed, wondering what she could possibly need, a published author who made her living as a ghost in the clouds.

DANTE'S GRILL

Yes, I did work at Dante's back in those days when you had to get a job with just enough money to pay rent for a room in a basement and a little extra left over. A teenager showed me the way to cook a basket full of fries, boiled in oil, with burgers sizzling lined on the grill. Dante wrote about levels, a map of his descent into hell. This one wasn't all bad. I lasted a few weeks until I found a café that was better, a step up, or so I thought.

The HISTORY of MOTOWN

For too long, I lived in a basement apartment in a tenement house. $175 a month for roaming spiders, a bed made out of a shot-down biplane, a kitchen seeped in layers of fish oil, etc. etc. But I can't be too cruel about it, because there I was, for too long, my mind stuck in the overwhelming grief for a friend who died and feeling like I was dead too, in that tomb. But I did write while I was there: The Sand Rivers, Salmon of the Future, Believing in Windows, the *COW* magazines and all the books: *The Creation of the World, Poems in Zoos, Lawn Veterans, The Shrinkers, Waterhouse, Paying For Water, The Last Frankenstein, The Time Has Come To Make All The Machines Fly, Tree Frog* and more poems and things. Still, it was hellish. I had this idea that some beautiful vision would materialize and drag me out of there. I was very wrong about that. It was a bad time, the only way out was to help myself. I was working washing dishes when a friend told me about a house in Ballard. Quickly, I went back to my underground room, dragged out my things and a mattress, stuffed everything into a VW and got caught by my landlord. We didn't leave on the best of terms, she looked like a furious Grand Old Opry. But I was free at last! The same old song began...Only two of us paid rent, we couldn't afford heat, it was dead winter. America invaded Kuwait and bombed Iraq. A huge snowstorm hit Seattle and buried us. We burned our couch and kept the oven open, always on, for warmth There was an artificial leg hanging in the window. I wrote three books. *Good Deed Rain, Fish Bicycle,* and *Water Everywhere*...Then Waldo went on the rampage, he told us he could channel plants and he took a bottle of wine and left to court the lead singer of Heart, tracking her down to her mansion, lurking outside her gates like a shadow. It was bad...I found out about another house, immediately I moved in. A blue carpeted bedroom, heat pouring out of a metal vent, blinking Christmas lights twined around Buddha statues. Food Giant was just two blocks away. I played records in the morning, drinking tea, petting the cat named Pearl. For a while it seemed almost calm. Spring arrived and I wrote the *Flora Rabinovitch* book and poems like "The Doghouse" read under the monorail at night.

HER COMFORT DISAPPEARED
in GREEN SMOKE

An artificial leg hangs in the window.
There used to be electricity for the strings of
Christmas lights and electric guitars
until everyone ran out of money to pay for things
(someone gave all our rent to a stripper)
and then it was down to survival of the fittest.
The stove door hung open and poured out heat
(someone slept at night in front of its 400 degrees)
until we were reduced to candles in the winter.
Construction sites supplied plywood for fires
and Misty the dog watched us burn the couch.
Her comfort disappeared in green smoke
except for a cushion she got to keep in the corner

MILES to GO BEFORE WE SLEEP

I found out all I ever knew about her in the short span of a week. In the cold winter, I had moved into what used to be her room. The relief of getting into a space of my own was so incredible, I just concentrated on the miraculous working of the heat vent and all the blue, soft carpeted floor space. Finally, I could rest. I didn't concern myself with who lived there before me. Though she left a few things in the closet which I discovered: a black and white xerox of an Aztec dancing skeleton and a jacket which fit me. One day I wore it to the bus stop and I stuck my hand in the pocket. A clear plastic hospital bracelet with her name on it. Then someone told me about her. She had just been released from the institution, also, barely twenty, she already had two babies and she was pregnant again (she didn't seem to care, she gave them up for adoption). And now, she was returning to the house for a week, before joining her parents down in Costa Rica. I wondered if she would want to stay in her old room, maybe I should give it back to her. I didn't want to upset her, I try to be kind to people who have swirled under. Monday, I dragged home from work, my hands stinging from chlorine and the cold and I opened the door and there she awaited. Her shaved head was glued closely to the TV screen, watching *Jeopardy*. It didn't seem necessary for her to know we were there in the room with her, but I said hello. For a long time before she arrived, I'd been thinking about that shadowland pulling at us like a whirlpool, how careful you need to be, but she had plunged herself into its river. The entire week all she did was watch the television, whatever was on. I would go to sleep and I could hear her bedded down in front of the glow, laughing on and on at *Ed McMahon's Star Search*.

IT COULD ONLY BE LOUD, with ELECTRICITY, in the DARK

Driving downtown, stuck at a red light, jammed in traffic, I blasted *Songs for Swingin' Lovers*. If I maintain a good volume, it's almost a time machine I'm in. Instead of here, I'm in 1953. Out the window of their blue car, a white haired man waved and asked, "What station is that?" I laughed at the strange American experience and said, "It's a tape." Naturally, I thought of him flipping through the dials, trying to find a lost sound, feeling like a stranger in a strange land. It takes excavation to find good music, it's supposed to be lost to us. "It's Sinatra with Nelson Riddle," I said across the distance to their car. They grinned back, agreeing, "You've got taste." They drove away with memory in their car, just like me and this is supposed to be my time. The light changed to green, I steered through the intersection with everyone navigating potholes. With an introduction like that it would seem that I am a man who only breathes the Savoy Ballroom. Woefully, it was not always so, I have a past to hide, I played a part in a terrible noise. Here, let me park with this picturesque view of the Space Needle, for what I'm about to admit is just as much a product of this canceled city. Now that it's quiet, just the rush of passing traffic, I can unroll my confession. He was fresh from the Emergency Room, he still had the bandage circles on his chest that had attached him through wires to an electrical kick-starter machine of some kind. His throat was raw from the stomach pump. Now that he was alive again, he was anxious to get to the club for the show. When the band Orange Lorax played, it didn't matter if the singer tremored from a near-death experience, nobody would notice. So we loaded the car with guitars, drums, wigs and mannequin parts, Chinese lanterns, Christmas lights, voodoo gourds, a broken Lite-Brite and other things too that would sparkle or jump dangerously with electricity. The club was next to a gun shop and there was parking in back. We found a place next to a bleached heavy-metal girl having a baby in her Pinto, waiting for an ambulance. It was the kind of omen we had to take as good, in order to push forward, onward, toward the waiting doors. Miraculously, they let us inside, so we piled the equipment next to the stage while another band played. The crowd was pitiful, a handful of friends of other bands, and a lone cowboy, horribly misplaced in his white hat with a row of bottles at the bar watching the silent TV sports channel. It's really almost indescribable what happened as Orange Lorax hit the stage, and I watched it all happen from the soundboard where I manipulated the colored spotlights into a seasick froth. I remember feedback, tortured screaming, a drum flying through the air, the orgy of humpback whales, someone in a grass skirt falling down. No, I would rather forget it, what went on is gone. The owner cut the power and the bright yellow houselights came back on and Orange Lorax ceased to exist. It could only be loud, with electricity, in the dark.

CUBE

His wife was a behemoth who insisted on wearing cowgirl outfits when she waitressed. He worked there at night, sweeping and mopping the floors of the café. Before her shift ended at 5 PM he came in and sat by the window. He had a notebook, he would draw while he waited for her to be done. I was busy heaving up the rubber floor mats into the dishwasher, or scrubbing the stove. One day, his notebook was left open on the table. I happened to take a look. It was a series of mad attempts to draw a 'three dimensional cube.' I remember drawing this in 3rd grade: start with one square, then draw a second square overlapping it, and connect the corners with lines. Voila! Yet this simple, geometrical etch alluded him entirely. Every attempt to draw it was crossed out furiously. He couldn't do it!

SHRUG

I was with Malcolm
when he turned the motor off
after a minute of silence
because suddenly he didn't know
how a thing called a car worked
slipping his mind gears so easily
the green metal covered wheels
shrugging like a flower in a field

SEPTEMBER 4, 1991

The Pacific Northwest is a long way from California and I want to go back driving by night. I like the way the stars hang over the freeway. Before I started, I filled the gas tank, checked the oil and went to Safeway where I picked up a glow-in-the-dark Creature from the Black Lagoon who stands on my dashboard and burns like a dim green monster bulb.

The DRAGONFLY

No, it wasn't quite dead, even though I found it
like a frozen thing in the mud next to the lake,
even though I had washed it off in the cool water
twice and carried it the long way back to my car
and put it on the dashboard with the other relics
and good luck symbols: the glowing Creature,
a waving green dinosaur, sage picked from off
the mountains, a Trucking For America patch,
books and stones from wild rivers. It looked perfect
there. Then it fluttered and buzzed like a little toy.
The sun must have awakened it. I wanted to keep it
but not if it was alive, not if it moved, brought back
to life like Egypt. Someone in a black pickup
pulled up on the sand nearby and fired a gun twice
at the rocks and trees on the other side. The shots
echoed up and down, startling birds and the clouds
were turning red against the sunset.

RABBIT

A backyard party we went to at night, those Japanese lanterns strung from the trees run above us to the house trellis. We were introduced to Rabbit. He stood under the kitchen light. I said hello and a few other things. Then I turned the channel and went somewhere else. Later, as the night wore on, I ran into Rabbit again. He was a footstep from the garden. Holy Mackerel! He *was* a rabbit! Big teeth, long face, droopy hair hanging like ears. With a grin, he stood next to the garden like he was guarding it.

The LITTLE BLACK CAT

The little black cat
you can't forget
tries his best
to wake you up

He won't go away
while you sleep
he turns into air

Like a spirit
he finds you
in your dreams

The CURSE TRANCE

Everything today behaved under a magical trance, some kind of spell was at work moving through the clouds, down across Seattle, moving like rain. It's something I've come to expect. This is something I recognize, like seeing a 3-legged dog, or 20 clowns ordering pizza, or being threatened by a dwarf woman in a devil suit. The variety surprises me sometimes, but the fact that it is happening is natural. I have been cursed. I just don't know why. Once I tried to escape it. I got in a car one summer and drove South. It caught up with me in Reno. A persistent hobo tried to sell me a machine that would turn steam into gasoline. He needed money for the patent and half of the riches would be mine but I escaped and kept driving, ending in California. More trouble at a Mexican restaurant with a boxing ring. A crooked promoter named Kid Ramone. I drove at night hoping to avoid trouble that way. I returned to Seattle again, to the waiting arms of my curse.

GASWORKS

Today I met the Thunderbird God who sleeps hidden in the thorns in a nest lined with glass bottles. Chicken Joe has to go to the hospital for blood poisoning. Red gets held up with a gun at the back of his head. Roy gets drunk and loses his backpack which holds everything he owns. Jim gets beat up by five teenagers at 4 A.M. Then Eddy prays in the morning and gets fined $10 for panhandling. Red comes home with three bottles. Ray finds a new backpack full of things. Yes, Gasworks is the last stand, the way you have to look at things, that life really simply is a series of losses and gains.

GASWORKS STARS

A street rapper named Ice Cream Cone. The chestnut tree. Chicken Joe and his pregnant girlfriend Karma. A dwarf in a devil suit, prodding with her pitchfork, "Hey thir!" Foreign exchange student invasion/ Yard Sale warzone. Tattoo maniac with speakers in back of van blasting the latest Alice Cooper. Bob, pronounced Bop, in a van. Streetlights going off, sprinklers going on. Fairy lights shining in the tree in the park. Blackberries. Blackouts. Public showers. Russian peasant women with steel teeth. Gasworks Free dinners. Parking overnight. Demon at Taco Time. Foodbank sugar overdose. The Thunderjug. The Phosphorous Walrus. Jocko's Heavy Metal Rockers. The Kiss of Death. A Whale Farm. The crows. Mars on Five Dollars a Day. Mars on a Good Day. Clowns in The Knarr at Night. Zeke the Hillbilly, overalls and beard. Police everywhere. The Asian Flu Virus. Vietnam Veterans. Highschool students attacking homeless at park. The Sorrow of the Entire Planet put in a Bottle. Living Under the Highway. Good Things Are Out of the Same Blue. Quality Used Bacon On Dry Ice. The Neighborhood Watch Captain. Ever Ready Batteries. Werewolves and Hobbits. Look Up At Mars. They were the things that were happening, it was all such a warp of reality that it was coming out strange. It was hard to live with any real sense of sanity and calm.

GOOD DAY TEA

The last time I drank Good Day Tea, which is
the cheapest tea you can get at Safeway in a box
with a hundred bags, I was staying at Gasworks.
Firewood from a construction site, I shared it
around a cold picnic table with the homeless crew.
The homeless way in Seattle is like the sundial
on the top of Gasworks hill, pictures set in a crazy
circle of metal, trying to make sense of it.

you'll have to accept that what happens is real

CHOCOLATE

After months of really being hungry
it made sense to finally go to the Food Bank
to fill out forms and stand in the poverty line.
We didn't have the luxuries of heat or cold
but they gave us a bag for people that way.
Those who find themselves in those shadows
get cans, bread, crackers, generic peanut butter.
It's not very nice but you don't complain.
Already we've forgotten so many good things.
Then our eyes nearly boiled over with delight.
There was candy and a gallon of chocolate milk.
Sweetness was a mirage that shimmered on the verge.
As fast as we could we went through the sugar,
unwrapped and opened and consumed all we saw,
so quick it made us sick like a mad fairground ride
that flew us right back into the night.

WALLS COULD BE WALKED THROUGH

I found The Professor in the parking lot one late night. Someone had abandoned him there. I picture a shady car escaping along the dark lake. I brought the kitten inside, he was frozen in shock. He wasn't afraid of water though, it warmed him, then he fell asleep inside of my shirt. The Professor returned slowly, day by day. I gave him the content life of a cat and he started to remember life and be interested in what surrounded him. But he couldn't live with me the way I was living at the time. I was a one-man nightmare of ghosts and things and flying machines. My friend took the lucky cat with him to a house on the coast. He could roam in fields next to the Pacific and when the sun went down, he could find home at night and see a bat circle in the living room blind turns, brushing the walls until its radar clicked on the open screen door and it escaped. There were birds and mice, dogs, horses, loud tourists and their motor scooters, owls in the black tree canopy over their rented house. Soon, my friend started to notice unusual things about the cat. Walls could be walked through, invisibility, anti-gravity leaps through the air, the power to control where it wanted to be. When my friend ran into money trouble, his books weren't selling, the house was taken over and he had to return to the city for a job. Of course, the cat hated being back in Seattle so one day he didn't return. I imagined him walking beside the highway and dusty country roads in rain, over bridges, finally returning to the sea.

The TELEVISION BODHISATTVA

I've been thinking about the Television Bodhisattva.
He was ahead of his time, going around America
enlightening. The first time I met him,
he was staying in a tiny silver trailer parked in
someone's driveway at night. We knocked on
the tin door and he opened up bright light.
There wasn't much room inside the trailer
filled up with a mattress and a big-screen TV.
When he invited us inside, we had to climb
over the thresh to see what he was watching.
Later on he stayed in our apartment up past
Capitol Hill. Bringing only a television with him
he would sit there spread out on the floor
like a candle slowly melting from its flame.
The antenna was rigged with aluminum foil
to get the reception he needed.
I was younger then and quick to judge
and I told him what I thought of all that
propaganda, but he replied so calm,
"It's all in what you choose to let in,
there's always something you can learn."

ROYALTY TOY COMPANY

He sent out his thoughts to her address, made his mind be like a bird that could follow a map to the street and apartment where she lived. A window formed in his imagination and there she was behind the glass. All the good in the world couldn't live up to that.

DECEMBER 11, 1992

When you're not looking, somehow she will just appear, out of the wallpaper or in the sound of an opening door. Don't go looking for her, don't set out everyday hoping and searching all the eyes. Occupy yourself with something else and sometime in the middle of all the revolving, it will happen. This morning I tried to think of other things, as I watched out the bus window at this town they've built after chopping down all the trees. McDonalds, Burger King, Taco Time, Mutual Bank, U.S Bank, 7-11, Chevron, Exxon. It's not a big town but they've squeezed in all these places and more. Then the town was left behind and we were on the freeway. An over-ramp soared up beside us and there, standing underneath in the grass was a coyote. The rust gray of its fur, the frozen bend of its body, and its stare going right through the traffic. It was making itself invisible to everyone but me.

The PRINCESS of SADNESS

The Princess of Sadness works among the magazines and junk food clutter colors. It's hard to believe a castle has lost its future queen to this place. Her eyes are two whale tears and only thinking about pressing buttons keeps her from crying and flooding the cardboard aisles. It was one of those winter days she was poured inside when he happened to appear and the sight of her opened him and changed him with a charged feeling to become the bringer of mercury flowers and saving grace. Did all the storybook knights find water that washed them away? Or did all the blue unfold waves to a long hidden joy? Every time he went to see her, he brought inventions wrapped in Egyptian linen, every time he saw her, their eyes held each other.

APRIL 18, 1994

She took the robot out of dark and stood it in sun.
Wonder. For a moment, she sighed, tried to hope
for the right thing to do. She stopped her fingers
against the rusted cold metal bolts. A globe twirled,
shadows played. Would the usual thing happen again?
How many times, she held her hands, must I learn
and learn the same again? The electricity sometimes
doesn't work. It might turn into ash, but she pressed
the buttons because, "Sooner or later my wish
will come true."

JUNE 10, 1994

Right now, I've been watching the trees
for signs of Spring. There's a maple on the way
to work, I've seen its winter gray claws turn into
green hands. Apples have ballooned over the path
purple lavender and the birds sing in branches
or on telephone wires. When Monday through
Friday arrives, I open to what I see around me,
before I shut myself inside from ten until five.
Clouds, sky, water, I catch sight of you from
windows.

HER SPELLS

I heard the witch crying under trees in the city.
Her black dress spread around her in maple shadows
her hands held up to her wet eyes. Her spells weren't
working for her to be this way, out of wishing power,
the candle light in her was going out. All the way out
she swirled as she changed into water. A dark
whirlpool cast into hollow. The tree dipped its
branches lower, a river from her pool curved
away across the weeds and cement. Into traffic
splashing cars, carrying litter, cigarettes and
paper cups. I put my hand in to stop her from
flowing away and my cold hand froze. Then
I was slipping and turning into river too.
The current pulled more of me under.
I wondered what can last longer
this new city river or me,
holding onto dandelions.

The OLD GOAT

On the way to the bus each dawn I walked through a field on a path dug in bracket and thorn. I waited for the appearance of the mythical beast in leaves and sure enough he would be there, torn above the old glass gourds of wine, inside a windowfull of vines. A long white beard and curling over horns and eyes like blue marbles sunk so deep in the dew.

CLINTON STREET

Run away to there
go on a bicycle
Sunday ritual
talk with a cup
coffee and music
played on vinyl

Take a break
sit outside in the rain
on a black metal chair
watch the traffic
slow for the sign

If a friend shows up
go follow the day

FILMING CARUSO

The idea arrived in the phantom light of 2 AM. A 50 watt bulb on a cord clicked on, notes were hurried down until they were done.

In the morning, I was at the café washing dishes. Think about the storyline while the machine keeps rolling out white plates and steam.

Not long after a forty cent meal from a box, I sat with a cup of coffee and explained to Mike, "The film is called *Caruso*." I stopped to let it sink in to another sip of coffee. Just the name should roll upon the air like thunder.

While I waited for my Director's reply, the waitress came by and I caught her arm,

"More coffee please."

She paused and dead-pan delivered, "Would you like to order any *food* with that?"

"No," I told her. "Coffee's fine."

She was slow about it though. While she poured by drop, I laid out the story-line across the table.

"Here it is," I said. "Read it and weep."

We saw our camera waiting for auction, numbered on a shelf with Bermuda souvenirs and radio-controlled toys. First we had to wait through the antics of fishing poles being sold by the cowboy calling from his cage above.

"What about this stereo?" his voice rodeoed. "Jim, turn that on, let the folks hear it."

A shriek of noise wouldn't stop.

"Jim, turn that off!"

We watched poor Jim struggle with the bent dials. He mumbled something up. The cowboy yelled on and on at him. The crowd sat in folding chairs, fanned the heat with folded magazines.

At last, Jim followed orders and unplugged the set. The charge died. Some neon signs were next to go before the cowboy finally ordered Jim to hold out the Super-8.

"Seven dollars!" I heard the Director shout.

Miraculously, that was enough. Everyone else was waiting for junk.

Black and white Super-8 film is a thing of the past. As of that day, we had bought the last of it. Whatever was left would have to be enough.

Filming began on a sunny day in the graveyard. We parked the borrowed car next to a slate colored wall and got out. Makeup was applied to my feet (cornstarch and water, dots of red ink) and I fitted the pig mask over my head.

It needed a retake to film the simple path of pig between cemetery stones; the Director was laughing and the camera shook like a candle landslide.

Painted on the wall was the Budget descent, figured in pennies. The minute we lost to laughter had cost us six hundred of them.

The next bright day was all railroad shots. Pitiful feet dragging shoes on the tracks. Some Mexicans pulled up chairs beside the blackberries to be entertained. The heat of the sun in the mask was unbearable.

At the mortuary, I was chased down the steps by a pale ghoul in a dark suit.

At the traffic roundabout, the Director risked his life leaning out of a circling car, camera rolling at 40 miles per hour. A Russian tourist slurred advice. A pigeon shadowed over the bricks in Chinatown where the missions were early dawn releasing the bleary back to the streets. A church service was interrupted to capture their slamming door on film.

I couldn't afford a nail for a prop, so I stole one from the hardware store. And more seconds and minutes were taken from the air.

For a moment we considered giving the reels to a someone somebody knew. There was a bathtub involved. Picture it with lion claws, a rusty ring, filled deep with chemicals and the seaweed kinks of our developing film.

In the end, we chose to run the Budget into the ground. Check enclosed, *Caruso* was mailed off in a yellow envelope with the imposing return address: MGM Jr. A couple of weeks would have to pass.

The news arrived fast as I pulled the last load of glass from the dishwashing machine. The Directo clawed at the screen door like a firefly. "It's here!" he gleamed.

Yesterday we had rented the editing equipment by posing as college students, tonight we could hammer out the film seam by seam. A little crank pulled the film through. Peering over his shoulder, I watched the smallest window reveal white leader, then black. Slowly, as if driven by Bela Lugosi in a cape, the black ebbed away, leaving the titleshimmering . . . *Caruso*.

Fevered, we strung the midnight basement room with clotheslines. Bit by bit, we cut lengths of celluloid and numbered them with tape. The story hung from spider webs. Sticking them all together into one roll took the moon a long journey towards Japan. By the phantom light again, we watched in awe: the fade into trees, cut to a rose in a garden, written *The End*.

STILL CREEK

It was no wonder I heard
the voices of Still Creek
up there deep in the woods
on the slope of Mount Hood
in the dark of night when
the fire died and the only sound
came from the motion of rocks
and moving water

In the STREAM

So what about all those jobs that took all that young time away from me? What do I recall of them? Didn't I tell myself they would be inspiration for my apprentice work as a writer? I went from a glass factory in New York City, to a parking garage, to flipping burgers in a dive named after an Italian poet. Then I was in a Mexican kitchen, working with the owner's mother.
At the end of a long day, while he sat counting receipts, I mopped the black and white checkerboard floor. Then two more café jobs, the next one started at dawn. After the morning rush, I would find the lead cook asleep on the dryer, under a pile of warm, clean aprons and towels. One time during his Dormouse routine, a huge bag of flour inched off the shelf above and burst on him. He became legendary after he stumbled out into the dining room covered in flour, white as a ghost. I guess all these events made their way into books like *I Can Only Imagine*, stories and poems. I was always in the steam of those dishwashing machines, with the pink stinging soap and bleach on my hands. Another couple jobs like that and I was in another city. That's when I knew those jobs were sailing out of sight. Someone started leaving notes for me above the sink.

The LOVE NEST

When we moved the bed
we loved in so many times
the floorboards were strewn
with pennies and dust
like a nest underneath

BACK to MEMORY

That takes me
back to memory
night flowers and birds
nesting in the eaves
rain and blankets
when the city
was our dream

A BABY

Here's how I remember the way it happened.
We were on bicycles, riding a bridge across
the Willamette River like we always did then
and she told me, "I'm going to the doctor…"
only said the way of someone about to open
a door leading to a garden where a flower
is growing beautifully.

The GREYHOUND

We spent the night at a friend's. Dawn barked
in the form of a purple and blue greyhound.
Its bulging eyes goldfished urgently while
its mouth opened and snapped. Bark!
"What do you want?" I bolted upright.
The sleek dog shuddered and took a few steps.
I seemed to recall a request to take the dog out
when nature called. I groaned and got up.
My bare feet hit the floor, "Let's go, dog."
Only after I stumbled to the front door
and opened it did I realize what I had done.
My friend's retired greyhound racer launched
off the porch to rocket down the street.
"Waaait!" I called. "Hey—!" I struggled
to remember the dog's name. The lope
and curve of its disappearance was
awe inspiring. Frightening. Thirty five
miles per hour on the loose. I had to chase it
in my undershirt past every cold sleeping
house in the neighborhood.

The $50 RABBIT

Who would have known what we paid
to get where we are, that desperate
on the other side of this counter
we signed over travelers checks
and he gave us a toy rabbit prize
for a list of houses and apartments
that might rent out to us

This is WHO

So this is who walks around at 2 AM
in the neighborhood all blacked out
except for the tall amber street lamps
spaced every block and a half
I'm out walking the baby
in charge of wide-eyed insomnia
when the leaves of the willow
rattle behind us and ahead
a rabbit darts over the street
silent as a dream going home
to sleeping home

OHIO TORNADO

It's on the way
piling the sky
into a wave
over the I.G.A

The radio
warned us
waist tall
sunflowers
spin and bend
petals milling
in the wind

I planted them
beside the kitchen
to grow and look in
but now, staring
at those clouds
approaching,
there is nothing
more than knowing
they would be
left outside
while the window
thrashed in rain

The KALEIDOSCOPE CAT

When we lived in Ohio, one green summer
a kitten appeared at our afternoon door.
All wobbly, it came right inside and seemed
to want to make itself at home. It didn't have
a collar and I supposed it may have been
walking miles to get to our place. I went to
the refrigerator and poured a bowl of milk.
It stumbled up and I scratched its mothy coat.
I was already going through a list of names.
That's about as far as this kitten got to joining
our parade. I was willing to overlook
the poor creature's terrible crossed eyes,
that only added to its charm, I thought.
It would always be a cat who couldn't
walk a straight line in a kaleidoscope world.
If only I could convince my wife. That was
the hard part, she didn't see the cracked magic
potential in that cat. As it turned out, I never
got a chance to try—there was a sound of
children at our door—they were looking for
their pet.

The OPENING ACT

In Ohio, the famous State Theater glows beside
Lake Erie. It has been open from Vaudeville and
the Depression to this very end of the 20th century.
A crowd of bright colors bent to the ticket windows
to pay twenty dollars each and go inside. What
brought us there too was the moth-like appearance
of The Smothers Brothers. Jostling among the senior
citizens for a while, we hoped for a white haired
scalper or tickets to fall somehow on marble floor.
When we were alone, everyone was deep inside
the theater watching the red curtains and gold
carvings, we decided to sneak in. Around the
corner, we found a gray service door propped
open with a little block of wood. I opened it
scarcely to allow us through and saw red uniforms
dressed like decoys weighted down in chairs
sitting in the hallway. Also, a man with thick glasses
spotted me and was bearing down like one of
Roosevelt's ancient steam-driven dreadnoughts.
I hopped backwards and scooped my wife's hand.
We hurried down the length of theater and around
into the parking lot. I looked back over my shoulder
and saw the door just beginning to open, slowly.
We were safe. A dangerous looking fire escape
clung to all the bricks running towards the roof.
We could hear applause washing inside the theater.
Past the next corner at the side of the wall, we
discovered a stage door there. We were so close
we listened to the heavily bolted metal and heard

the familiar guitar and bass and voices from records.
I put my hand on the door and for a few seconds
considered what would happen if I opened it.

A GARAGE in OHIO

Every time we went
to the landlord's house
to pay our rent
we saw where
our money went

tall white pine
beside the garden
boards moving up
beams and walls
built with our help
getting bigger
every month

The 1940s

A long time ago in Ohio I worked
at an old brick red public library.
I met the author of the town
when grade school let out.
He was very prolific already,
I think there was something
in the rusted water, the fields
shot through with pesticides:
maybe all of it inspired him.
This 7th Grade boy showed me
a detective book he wrote.
The manuscript was bound
in a folder colored a purple shade,
perfect for that old black and white world.
I still remember the first sentence:
"It was the 1940s and everyone
dressed well."

STATE FARM

One Ohio morning driving to work
with one headlight working the fog,
a police car had to get me. Luckily,
he fell for the fake insurance card I photocopied
with the year skillfully blurred by a crease.
But I realized how slim the chance that charm
could work again. We needed real insurance.
In defense of that crime, let me explain
the reason was money—a half time job in
a library doesn't pay more than rent and food.
We barely made it every month.
After calling numbers in the yellow pages
I found an old man and we went to his house.
He overlooked a lot of things he must have known.
Just looking through the cloudy white curtains,
he could see our car parked next to flowers
in his driveway. Our situation was understood
without needing explanation.

The ½ CREATURE

It was prairie, all yellow colors.
The highway exits onto a road
that turns into dirt that leads
to a gas station.
We were on the way
back from Ohio.
I got out of the cab.
It was cold and quiet
except for the rush of traffic
on the interstate beyond.
Inside the store I paid
for a full tank and bought
a refrigerator magnet
a Jackelope, that creature
native to this land,
half rabbit/half antelope.
Carrying it, staring at it,
I half believe it's real.

A FACTORY JOB

When we were new to this town, I tried the papers
for work every morning for a week. Then I guess
I got desperate. I went to a temp agency on lower
Holly Street where the creek ducks under the city
bridges and spreads into tide. A couple other people
in there with me and while we filled out applications,
they played a horror movie on the TV.
I got placed at a factory north of town along I-5.
It was so loud we had to wear earplugs all day.
I stamped metal to make mufflers for semi trucks.
On my lunch break outside, I could see them drive by.
My work was going right into all that speed and noise.
I was there until I found something better and quieter.
Work in a library. Even after all these years when
we happen to take the interstate up that way, I look
for that low building but it's gone, or I can't remember
the way and I don't doubt that's a good thing.

The BICYCLE TOMB

We came home to find a man with a broken foot
clawing through the boxes in our backyard shed.
It wasn't something I wanted to see, or the yellow
lopsided truck in the alley. He muttered the word
for bicycle—he forgot it in there when he used to
rent this house. Behind the wall of dead cardboard,
the Edgar Allan Poe of bicycles was a frightening sight.
All rust and broken ribs and bends and tangled over
with black veins of dead berry thorns. He clubbed
his tragic mummy foot over the stones unsteadily
with the bicycle in his arms. I put it in the truck bed
for him. It wasn't much, it must have meant more
in memories.

SLOW LEAK

It doesn't help
having a boss like her
riding you all the time
from eight to five
week after week

She lets out the air
living inside you

And it takes hopes
going home and dreams
to find the strength
to start over again

FRANKLIN LILACS

One time I was returning from work
down Indian Street up to the corner
past the credit union, finally around
the lilacs on Franklin Street,
another left turn and a right
and next to the old church steeple
there's our house by the willow tree.
Some people are out on lawns
looking at the sky. I noticed it too:
a silver thing hovering like a kite.

RIVER STONES

We drove the winding road towards Mount Baker
tall trees, little farms and houses carved out of green
watching for a sign tucked along the road.
Seeing it, we slowed and turned into a driveway
all gravel rutted by the rain. There was a trailer
with a truck stopped next to it. We parked there.
Our 8 year old daughter spent last night out here.
We could hear the river nearby. We stood next to
our car, listening when the trailer door opened.
"They're out there playing," said the woman in
the bathrobe. So we followed the path pointed
towards the sound of rushing water. We ducked
under branches, went down a dirt embankment
onto stones and a muddy delta shape the water
went around. We had to hop a trickling stream
to land on it. The woods filled all around us,
we were just in this small space, on the stage
in a fairytale. There were little white flowers
growing, green shoots and leaves, tiny birds
hopping. We left footprints looking for theirs.
They weren't hard to find. Their voices carried
from the river on the other side of a hill.
They were playing some loud game,
both girls carrying plastic bottles of lemonade.
Their eyes were wild-looking as tumbled
river stones. As we walked them back
our daughter explained, someone had seen
a mountain lion yesterday and they were
out in the woods looking for it.

On a WET CORNER

On a wet corner
a traffic light shines
in the night rain
we all know
it's late
we feel
what's
going on
waiting
for
everything
to change

KING MEDICINE

I suppose it turned into a bit of a story after all, going to Bangor to see the Stephen King house. It's one of those things I just had to do. If I was in Memphis, Tennessee I would feel the same way about Graceland. I would have to go. I would stand in front of that metal gate just like the tourists do. First we stopped at the Brunswick library to get a book on CD. I chose *Cell* because I knew the way it just ripped right into story. Pulling out, we passed a man in a pink shirt, smoking a pipe and I threatened to take him along with us. 295 North was a good drive, like a painting, calm smooth new black tar, little traffic, low pines on either side. CAUTION MOOSE signs and after a long while listening to *Cell* and my daughter's occasional gasps, the garbage hill before Bangor. It looks like a weird mountain the road bends for and misses. Of course I thought of the paper drafts that might be in there. I know I've thrown my share of stories away. We took Exit 184 and waited to go right on Union Street. A beefy man with a Boston Red Sox t-shirt shuffled in the crosswalk. We passed Mansfield Stadium a little later and saw the stands full and I thought he's probably there. We missed West Broadway and I had to turn onto Pond, then Cedar and I could feel we were very near. I knew it was a red house. Suddenly it jumped out at me. Well, it was easy to feel like a fool now but I had to do it. The street was eighty feet wide, mansions on either side and nobody was parked nearby. I pulled over just past the property corner with a big green frog statue. I don't know what I expected to happen—no, I do—I can tell it in awful truthfulness: Like any other fan drawn here, I expected there to be a chance of this happening: at just this moment, Mr. King would be coming out, a wave, I could say hello and talk a minute. Meanwhile, Grandpa made a call on his cellphone to tell where we were, put his cell away and shambled at Rosa like a zombie along the curb. We got our pictures taken awkwardly. All the windows looked still and I couldn't blame them. I could hear shrieks from the baseball field a couple blocks away. We got back in the car, but I wasn't done yet. I had to try the stadium. I could picture him there, in the bleachers, watching the game. What a bizarre ride we were on. A potbellied man on the corner of Hammond wearing shorts, black socks, with an umbrella tucked under his arm. All day long a fog had clung to the trees. The radio kept warning us about a hurricane. That fellow was prepared. Past the Dead River Company, we circled those streets back onto 13th and then we were there. I pulled off of the road and stopped on the grass with the other cars. I was the only one who dared to get out. "But look…" I said, pointing to a man on the other side of the mesh wire fence. He sat at a picnic table, writing something. "That might be him, right there." When I got closer, walking past all the rows of parked cars, I could tell it wasn't him. The announcer inside set up another batter, a strange sounding name, and people clapped in the tall stands. I went around to the gate and read Senior World Series and the admission cost, 10 dollars. That stopped me. I turned around. I went back to the car. Now I just wanted to get a postcard to send. Do I need to say how I even failed at that? The Family Dollar store didn't have any, the grocery no, nor the gas station where there was a dwarf in front of me in line. "I'm sorry dear," the cashier said. It's a winding and steep river town, old buildings, iron, stone, wooden, people living in a dream. We saw the Paul Bunyan statue, giant maniac face that I've read about. I didn't really expect to write this, I didn't take notes the way I should have. We drove out of there, over the Penobscot again, heading south on Route 1, caught in tourist traffic, a taste of my own medicine, slowed to a crawl for every tourist town from then on, Camden, Rockport, Waldoboro, Damariscotta, Moody's Diner, Wiscasset on down.

SEPTEMBER 24, 2010

The History Channel called me today. A woman doing research for a show on velocipedes found out through the vast internet colossus that I wrote a book called *Velocipede*. Unfortunately, I let her know that's an unpublished novel. A character works at a factory making them. She laughed, we hung up. A swimming pool and platinum Hollywood pearls seep through my hands.

A LIVING by WRITING

Really aren't I making
my living by writing anyway?
I'm here at my job but
the real work of writing
comes throughout the day
and lays down in pages
so I can say that I am
being paid for being
a writer, even though
nobody knows it.

The JOURNAL of The MERMAID TRANSLATION, part 1

I have a box filled with my new novel, *The Mermaid Translation*. I wasn't going to write about this, but now it seems I am. I'm not sure if it's a diary, in order to keep my own astounded observations, or simply a look at what happens when you begin to write. Anyway, let's just call it a journal. And it's a good place to start, with this cardboard box of books.

On Saturday, I put it off as long as possible, until finally, after 3 o'clock I pushed myself into action, grabbed a book from the box, the car keys and family and out the door we went. It was raining, dark—dreary is the word—but I had to hope the weather was not a reflection of deeper meaning. First stop was the public library. I parked and left with Rustle in the back dancing to Elvis Presley. These things take enormous nerve. I'm not fond of doing this at all, but onward I charged.

The librarian had just finished talking up the books on the new-release shelf and she turned to me with a smile. I asked her about using one of the rooms for a reading. She showed me the rental fee. I guess that was enough for me. Part of the fantasy I have is that people (I mean libraries and bookstores) would be excited about having a local author read in their place. It just isn't like that. Unless I was J.K Rowling Jr. They want the money. I went in the rain back to the car. And on to the next stop.

My favorite bookstore in town sits on a slope with old trolley tracks and the rain running down. Years ago, they used to be on the corner of Harris Avenue; we used to go there all the time when our daughter was a baby. Their new store is beautiful orange wood, looking out over the bay. Just before I went inside though, I swore and slammed the car door. My wife didn't believe they wouldn't accept copies of my book to sell. After the library and in fact *years* of doing this sort of thing, I know better. Still, I held to a golden thread of hope that this wonderful dreamy bookstore would be different. But I told her I knew what they were going to say. And she scolded, "See, you're just going to make that happen." My rude reply was, "XXXX!" and "Just watch what happens..." So I fumed out of the car with the new book tucked beneath my sweater. Through the rain and yellow light, I got to the counter and explained that I am a writer living in this town and this is my new book. I'm trying to get it reviewed in the local papers. I am hoping I can mention that copies are for sale here. (There would be hordes of people arriving after the glowing reviews.) She soured immediately, "I'm afraid we have too much overstock, our inventory couldn't handle another book." Okay, okay, I said. I honestly didn't expect it and I'm sure it sounded bad when I softly told her it was my favorite bookstore.

Outside, the family was moving on, ahead of me, following the sidewalk to where it fell apart and turned into gravel and weeds. I caught up at a puddle and we went to the big bookstore rising over the street. Voltage Books is the place everyone goes, the place everyone thinks of first. Unfortunately they've become notoriously heavy-handed when dealing with small press books. To sell books here, the author needs to provide complimentary copies and any sold are subject to a 60/40 split. So actually I'm losing money trying to sell my books. On top of that, they charge the author a ten dollar fee to give a reading. So, with the library letting me down, and my favorite bookstore failing me, my confidence was at lowtide as we went in. Right away I noticed Robert at the cash register. I let the string of customers wind past, then I said hello. He's always been a good egg. I handed him the new book and muttered I'd like to do a reading. Robert flipped through it, "Oh, you should..." he said, "You *have* to do a reading." He called someone on the intercom but she wasn't around, so he wrote down a couple of contact names. One of them I already wrote to last week. I thanked him, I had become so flustered I told him the book was for him, I even signed it. At this point I didn't know what I was doing anymore. He seemed pleased with it though. As I left, he told the woman next to him, "This is the third book of poetry someone's given me this week." Yeah, I believe it. We're just throwing it to the wind.

Yesterday I mailed a copy of the book to another Robert. My friend Rob is a musician who lives in Seattle. He wants to record people reading it, then drone the results at an art gallery. It sounds fun. This weekend we might try to meet at a studio. In the meantime, a good review of sorts—my 5 year old niece in Ohio got a copy of the book. Maya refuses to part with it. When she isn't carrying it with her, she keeps it in a wooden box like a holy relic. Her mother had to wait until Maya was asleep to slip it from her hands so she could read it.

And that right there brings up the most maddening thing about writing these books. The problem is knowing that it's good and unique, but it's written for the appreciation of another time. I am coming to understand that but it's still hard. It would be nice in this life to make a living from it, but I think of those wandering poets of China and Japan who wrote on cliffs and leaves and bark hundreds of years ago. Now they're translated, carried in pockets, on subways and satellites. Today I'm going to mail a book to my friend Michael. He would understand what I'm talking about too. For years he's run his own small press. Many moons ago we worked together in a warehouse, that's where I got to know him. That's when he showed me a book that changed my life, a small novel that was designed like a Big Little Book, with text on one side and a drawing on the other. I carried that book and read it everywhere until it was done and I returned it to Michael. It immediately affected the magazine I self-published (*Pie in the Sky*) and I kept it in the back of my mind until I wrote *The Heaven Antenna* in Ohio in 1997. In fact, the original book (which was later published as *The Ohio Trio*) was handwritten with text and drawings in honor of that book Michael showed me. However, in the years that poured past, I forgot the title of that magical book. I guess I figured it was a one-of-a-kind underground flower. But I recently contacted Michael again—he's living on an island near Oregon now. He reminded me: *The Great Canadian Sonnet*, by David McFadden. So I gladly sent Michael my new book—if it hadn't been for him, I don't know how my writing would look.

Just emailed two local newspapers, *The Bellingham Herald* (which of course features in my book) and *Cascadia Weekly*, asking if I could send them copies of the book to review.

The Herald responds:
"We don't do book reviews, but we do publish author events and occasionally interview an author in conjunction with an event (usually at Voltage Books). When you have a reading, let me know, and maybe bring by a copy of your book for consideration. Thanks."

No response from *Cascadia Weekly*.

This morning Paul Piper leaned out his window into the rain to yell at me, "Hey Allen Frost, you're famous! I just ordered your book from Amazon!"

Every day, do something to keep it in motion. Today I printed out a 6 page list of all the libraries that own copies of the other 4 books I have published. Next, I need to find the time to go over them, get addresses and send them flyers for the new book.

Sent two emails. One to Rebecca, telling her I have a book for her. She's appreciative; she came up one day out of the blue and told me she had my first book. She had been to my reading at Voltage Books so many years ago when it came out. A few weeks ago, she traded me a bag full of homemade cookies for *Bowl of Water*, my second book.

Also, sent an email to Vowels bookstore in Portland, Oregon, hoping to set up a reading there. That would be wonderful—a chance to go back to the city where I landed in 1995, barely on my feet, worked as a dishwasher, met my wife—a city of memories and poems.

Trip to Seattle didn't quite work out the way I hoped. No recording done, but I did get to hear Rob's ideas for his show—the *Mermaid* book would be heard as a murmuring, coming from filing cabinets in a dark room lit only by little bedside lamps. I like it.

Sunday, we went to see the exhibition at the Seattle Center—the lampposts wearing colorful banners leading to the doors, a big line of people buying tickets, some fans lucky enough to rent hand-held recorders narrated by the author. Waiting to go in, waiting to see the original props, accessories and wardrobes from the book. "Marvel at all the handcrafted detail you will see surrounding you," promised the barker. Buzzing in the line with adults, teens and children, finally going in through the doors, shutting us inside a black room with blue rippling wave lights projected on the ceiling. A mermaid in a tank of water announces, "Welcome everyone to *The Mermaid Translation Exhibition*!" After a burbling fanfare, the curtains on the right of us part to reveal a green and blue light shining through a round porthole door. All on its own, the door opens wide into a gasping sight of a beautiful summer meadow. "It's Sanford's yard!" someone yelps and we all step in. Yes, behind the ropes of our path is Sanford's bathysphere. Wildflowers cushion it, you can almost reach out and touch it. A huge model of an elephant looms out, a red balloon sits in the air, you can faintly hear the piano playing. There's the periwinkle shell of the mermaid's café, follow the crowd inside. All the cups are hooked, a stove with pots of tea and coffee in a copper urn, the rippling moat the mermaid pushes through, the wooden tables and chairs, the lighthouse pearl turning, the jukebox with the record "How To Speak Dolphin" nested on it. Look over there! It's the actual tiger suit worn by Jenny! And standing next to it, the elegant tuxedo and top hat ensemble of the magician. Suddenly, on guide-wires overhead, a flock of yellow canaries flickers by. In a glass case are Mr. Merrimac's prop books, along with worn telephone books and the torn-out page listing Penny Certain Recordings. "Emily Dickinson's bread!" A phone booth, a dunking booth, the Saturn Circus sign, with two skeletons guarding the gate. The mood is calmer in the set of the poet's shack. The floorboards creak. Look out the window, across the cattails and birdsongs, see the sun reddening, going down. The autoharp, candles and soup cooking in a pot. On the wall of the hall leading to the next exhibit are movie posters faded and colorful. *Octopus Attack* and publicity stills and tattered circus handbills. Walk through a shining gondola car, in one door, out the other, into Mr. Dash's observatory. Standing amid tropical plants are the clothes worn by the book's characters. People laugh and point at Denton Pine's worn tweed suit, posed as if on the run from the librarian. Sanford's little clothes hold a lantern in each hand. Out from there, we follow a rocky mining tunnel that drops us right into the gift shop.

Email from Vowels bookstore:
They forwarded my request for a reading on to "our marketing team."

2 emails from my publisher, Larry Smith:
"I'm nominating *The Mermaid Translation* for a Pushcart Prize. I don't think we've ever had anyone win, but it's great to be nominated."
&
"I opened my email to find each of the Amazon.com warehouses ordering *The Mermaid Translation*. This is good. Some are ordering 6, some 2. About 20 in all. Whoopee! They had asked me for a 'forecast' list of publicity for the book, and I told them of ads to come out and readings planned or in the works. It works."

Response from Voltage Books:
They have a new consignment agreement since the last time I read there. It now costs $25 (up from $10) because "consignment is very time-consuming to manage." Also, they want me to provide 5 copies

of the book. The only bright note: they referred to the book as "Mermaid in Translation," which is kind of interesting.

Response from Vowels bookstore:
"Thank you for your email. I appreciate your willingness to present your new novel at one of our stores, but I unfortunately don't think we would see the size audience or sales to support an event and must decline."

I realized something about *The Mermaid Translation*. Not only is it a sort of cartoon, like a Saturday morning one with an undersea hero, it's also like a dream the way it seems so serious when you're in it. Then, when you awaken, even as it's fading, you wonder what all the running and worry and story was for?

November 15, 2010—November 24, 2010

The JOURNAL of The MERMAID TRANSLATION, part 2

In what could prove to be an action-packed development *The Mermaid Translation* was processed by the library today, to be shelved in the current display area. A cataloger asked me if it should be cataloged as poetry or fiction. "It's a novel," I said. But is it? I guess. Anyway, it will be interesting to see if the book makes any waves here. After all, this very library is featured in the book.

Compiled a list of 55 libraries that have my other 4 published books in their collections (California, Maryland, Indiana, Texas, Maine…). Will mail them flyers—the old fashioned way, in an envelope with a stamp.

Sent *The Herald* news about the reading, set for Friday, December 17th.

Email from my tireless publisher:
"We have an ad for *T.M.T* coming out in January issue of *American Poetry Review*…I've posted that it's nominated for the Pushcart Prize. Let the word spread…"

Looked for the book in the library catalog and discovered that it's been listed as being in Government Information, second floor. That can't be right. Looks like they might have made a cataloging error after all.

Received a bag of cookies and lemon cupcakes from Rebecca in trade for the new book. What a deal. I didn't even make it back upstairs to my desk before I had to have a treat. Delicious. With any luck, things will go back to trading. Would you like a book? That will be one pie and a kiwi fruit.

Pushing the book cart, I stopped to talk with Paul Piper. He told me about this new wondrous spiritually enlightened dental assistant he has, with the calming touch of an angel. (The complete opposite of my last dentist visit when the assistant stabbed herself with my Novocain needle.) Paul told his assistant she inspired him to write a story. Sure, I said, his character would be so smitten with her that he would do all the wrong things to get back in her dentist chair again—slurp sugar soda by the gallon, chew metal, whatever it took to return to her. Paul said he would leave that story twist to my version of the story. He suggested we do simultaneous stories based on the same event and see how they turn out. Interesting idea.

Took our son to a birthday party today, a block away from Voltage Books. Staring at that bookstore felt strange and I didn't want to go in there, close as we were. The party was in a big room above the Teapot Café. Rustle was greeted by the birthday girl. She's 7. Her mother introduced herself. I did likewise then put an arm around my daughter's shoulders and said, "And this is my wife." Rosa is 13. The woman was truly shocked! You could feel she believed it was true. I've been noticing this trend lately: my humor has been bombing pretty badly. Even though I assured the birthday girl's mother I was joking, she practically pushed us out the door.

Email from my publisher:
"I had a review copy request from a guy who does a national blog…also does listing on Good Reads. I'm sending it out Monday."

Put 12 envelopes in the mailbox for libraries stretching from Arizona to Iowa. Pulled up the rusted red flag. Watched out the window later as the little white truck arrived and drove them away.

At 6 o'clock tonight *The Herald* called. The lady on the phone was adding the date of the reading to the paper's event listings. But she needed to know the title of the novel. I guess I forgot to mention that part when I contacted them.

Note from Rob in Seattle:
"Worrying over a title for this thing. I kind of want to call it 'Penny Certain Recordings.' Where did you come up with Penny Certain? Not sure. Something that connotes memory...remembering. I recorded a bunch of passages from it today and some sound effects and other things...it is a lovely book! Nice butler! And I love the homing pigeon intercoms."

Today is our son Rustle's birthday. I made a big paper 7 to hang from the ceiling and left into the dark stormy early morning. At work, the water is out. A city water main was broken. By 10 it's been repaired and the sky is clear too. Blue sky, clouds blown away. I write a quick note to author Tom Robbins inviting him to the reading.

Mailed 9 letters to libraries from Iowa to Maryland.

Mailed 8 letters to libraries from New Jersey to Texas.

Email from another Robert:
"I'll be there! By the way did you know that a circus elephant escaped captivity back around 1910 and established a brief residency in Whatcom Creek near the spot where it crosses under Cornwall Ave? A huge field where Bellingham High School is now was the site of the circus every year." [Note: Loyal readers will recognize this as the inspiration for my novel *Roosevelt*].

Submitted a short story "Aristotle's First Car" written quite a while ago, but still waiting to be published. It's part of a big short story collection I'm hoping will be my next book.

Note from my publisher:
He and his wife went to Oberlin "to see a film in the Apollo, stopped by Mind Fair...and there it was...up on the wall in the front window." I can't get my book into the bookstores in my hometown, but farover in Ohio, people walking along the street can look in and see.

With the help of a *Sub Mariner* comic, I collected 4 selections for audience participation at reading on Friday night. (Other 3 pieces are from Steinbeck's *Sweet Thursday*, a poem by Robert Sund, and some Raymond Chandler from *The Big Sleep* when Marlowe meets the General in his greenhouse.) Hopefully there will be at least four people in audience and four who will agree to read.

Email from J. Genius:
"Wow. The title & the cover are a knockout. I can't wait to enjoy your new book! The soul needs sustenance. If you'd like to do some audience participation please feel free to count me in. I am, after all, 3 parts ham."

Sent off two poem submissions "Who Wouldn't Want a Gorilla Mask?" and "We Live Beneath."

18 The Bellingham Herald Thursday, December 16, 2010

Calendar whatcom

LITERARY ARTS
Allen Frost
Friday, Dec. 17, 6:30 p.m.
Ayurvedic Health Center,
Bellingham, 203 W. Holly
St.; Free; 360-752-9682
Local author Allen Frost will read from his fifth book, "The Mermaid Translation," a fantastical novel set in a circus-run Bellingham.

Found out there's an appointment at the office scheduled right after the reading. Will have to keep it under 45 minutes. I think I have it all put together, I just need to time it.

🐚

Coming back from walking the dog I checked the mailbox and lo and behold, there's a letter from Tom Robbins! Looks like he won't be making it to the reading, but it was great to hear from him.

Had the reading last night. We went to the office a half hour early, I put a sign out on Holly Street and we set up the rooms—an urn of chai tea, cookies, the 5 books for sale, also an extra box if hordes of people show up. The kids were playing Harry Potter, as usual, until Rustle needed my help finding the bathroom. We walked down the hall. The walls have never stopped smelling of paint. The Clover is an old building, a fantastic thing with 3 floors, creaky tipped hallways that looks like a set from *Outer Limits*, filled with odd offices, paper nametags on doors: travel agencies, restaurant supply, tax advice, or just a mysterious word. When Rustle was 2 or 3 he loved elevators—the Clover has a great one—and once he slipped away down the hall and got in the elevator by himself. We caught up with him on the next floor, his eyes wide. So I was taking him towards the Executive Suites sign when J. Genius appeared. "Yes," he observed, "You look like a father taking his son to the bathroom." Afterwards we went back to the office which had collected a few more people. A woman was apologizing before taking off her shoes, "My sock has a hole in it." "That's nothing…" I replied and held up my left heel for inspection. The whole back of my foot was exposed, the way it usually is, the reason I get cold feet walking to work in my sandals. There used to be two little girls from Vietnam who would wait with their mother at the bus stop. They noticed and would laugh at my feet. I thought about turning that into a poem. A few more people showed up and found chairs. When it was 6:40 and I guess around 12 people (the audience was all people we knew, no sign of *The Herald* readers, no cigar chewing kid from Chapter 16) *The Mermaid Translation* began.

Our dog started barking this morning, not unusual with her nose pressed to the window pointed towards the street. A yellow checkered taxi was parked at the curb, a guy in a thick black coat was getting out. He held a suitcase and he had a cardboard poster tube tucked under his arm. I've never seen him before. I brought the dog into the kitchen, she was still carrying on, but when I got back to the window, the taxi was pulling away, leaving fog and the visitor was walking up the driveway. He got past the sign on the gate 'The World's Smartest Dog' and then there was a knock on the door.

"Hello?"

"Hi, my name's Darp Thiggens," it sounded like he said. It was cold out there on our doorstep, it seemed like it might even snow. "I'm from Kazow Toys. They sent me here to speak with you in person."

"What about?"

"We're interested in turning *The Mermaid Translation* into a board game. I've brought along some blueprints."

"Alright," I said. I let him in. I closed the door, even though he had the air of a salesman. They do try our house from time to time, paying no attention to the dog sign on the fence or the warning 'Solicitors Butchered!' posted on the porch.

He set the suitcase down and tapped out the blueprint scroll. So even though he mentioned my book title, I was half expecting him to try and sell me a collapsible broom, or a willow rotor. But when he unrolled the paper and held it up, I saw something else: a map of a town beside the ocean, a circus on the bay, a hill with a mansion at the top, and mines underneath everything. Looping through it all was a path like the yellow brick road. Leaning closer, I could see the familiar characters from the novel drawn as little moveable game pieces.

"That's the blueprint," he said and laid it on the chair. Then he unlatched the suitcase. With a flourish he presented, "And this is the working model…"

Mesmerized, I watched as the little plastic figure of Sanford rode the gondola string up the cardboard slant of September Hill.

11/30/10—12/18/10

The JOURNAL of The MERMAID TRANSLATION, part 3

12/20/10

After the reading J. Genius and I were talking about one of the legendary tragedies of poetry, Samuel Coleridge's writing of "Kubla Khan." Of course the story goes that Coleridge was in the midst of poetic ecstasy, transcribing the lines direct from the ether, when his assistant bumbled into the room, ruining the transmission. The following Monday, I read J. Genius' book review:

"Hey, I read all the way up to the LAST PAGE of *The Mermaid Translation* last night—was loving every beautiful, breathtaking, freshly imagined detail...I still haven't read the final page. How will I ever re-create the wonderful mood of relaxation and wonder I enjoyed, anticipating Sanford's final moments. The passage about the blind canaries removing Emily Dickinson's bread from the Chinese Coal Miner's Curse, is freaking amazing. Loved that. Good medicine for the soul. Ah yes. It's providing much needed doses of beauty and creativity at this stressful juncture in my "professional" life. Another chapter I really enjoyed was the one where the old guy is carrying drapes and laundry down the street and a gust of wind carries him away. That was a lovely vision."

12/20/10

Letter to Seattle's Poetry House:
I'm an author of poetry, stories and novels living

up in Bellingham. I have just published my 5th book, a novel entitled *The Mermaid Translation*. I was wondering if it's possible to send you a copy to see if you'd like to host a reading of the book? Thanks for your help,
Allen Frost

1/3/11

The short story I submitted last month "Aristotle's First Car" was rejected. I don't keep those rejections or look at them again combatively (contrary to the young Stephen King who would impale them onto a rusty nail in his attic). Nevermind. This story will find a home in the short story collection I hope to publish next. It will be a wonder.

1/3/11

Email from my publisher:
"Ad is out for your book in *American Poetry Review* Jan/Feb. issue...should draw some attention."

The Mermaid Translation

by Allen Frost

A Poet and fiction writer from Bellingham, WA, Allen Frost delivers his 4th book with Bottom Dog Press/ Bird Dog Publishing

"This is one of those wonder books of old in the tradition of William Blake, Kenneth Patchen, and Richard Brautigan. It's a magic fable. A novel in poetry." -Larry Smith

978-1-933964-40-9 140 pgs. $15

1/7/11

That letter writing campaign is working—2 more libraries have added *The Mermaid Translation* to their holdings—University of Notre Dame and New York Public Library. Bravo!

1/14/11

Just mailed off a copy of *The Mermaid Translation* to a Hollywood director. [Note: It was Tim Burton! Was hoping for *Big Fish* treatment. Never heard back though.]

1/24/11

Sent off a story submission: "Abandoned Television Stars." Good luck, Captain.

1/24/11

Who would have thought it would be so hard to find a postcard? (Actually, I recall the same difficulty in Bangor, Maine when I searched in vain at a grocery store and a gas station.) On Saturday afternoon we walked to the Food Pavilion. They used to have postcards near the front doors but now it's just flowers and newspapers. We passed the mail truck on the way home so I still had time if I could find a card somewhere. I rode the bicycle to the other grocery store down the road. It took about ten minutes. I asked a steely-eyed guy in a green apron for help in my quest. He gave me a suspicious look, then told me no. Oh well, I bought flour and a can of peaches instead. Next door, I tried the drugstore. They used to have spinning racks full of postcards. Once there were flocks of them to be seen. But I walked up and down aisles to no avail. A cashier pointed and told me, "We have some postcards at the end of Aisle 11." Well, it wasn't surprising I missed them. They had 5 designs. The only one of Bellingham was a badly composed blue ship sticking out of the land. I couldn't buy that. I figured that was it, then I remembered the college bookstore around the corner, down the sidewalk. I got there just as they were closing for the day. They did have some cards and I gave them a look. There were no regional cards at all, so I chose a bright orange painting of a woman in Africa. As I stood waiting at an empty cash register station, a family walked by and a boy sneezed on his sister. She was yelling at him while they left. Someone hurried from the back of the store and rang up my sale. Outside, I found a bench where I could sit next to my bike and write. Why did I go to such a grand effort, 4 different stores, in search of a postcard? I just wanted to thank the bookstore in Ohio for displaying *The Mermaid Translation* in their front window. Isn't it strange and a little sad that postcards are on the way out? I thought so, riding back home, still hoping to catch the postal truck at some point. Fortunately, there it was, just across the street, parked in an abandoned restaurant lot, beside a wall of graffiti. I pulled up next to it and waved the card at the driver who was taking his break. Lucky he was there. I was happy to see my thanks go to Ohio, stamped on a colorful postcard, mailed from miles away.

1/24/11

Message from Rob in Seattle:

"I was just selecting a few more paragraphs from T*he Mermaid Translation* to read today for my 'installation.' It is a great book and my project won't do it justice. [Editor: Not true!] Sorry, kid but thems the breaks."

1/25/11

It seems it didn't go too far, but then the Titanic never reached her destination either. *The Mermaid Translation* rests just offshore in Bellingham Bay. Sometimes on a quiet night, you can hear her ghostly bell ring in the current. People like to tell haunting stories: does the ship's band really play on mournful moonlit high tides? Divers can swim overhead and see the murky rise of smokestacks and the radio tower. Schools of fish and wreckage. It's become a child's seaside rhyme to throw in a dandelion life-ring for the souls who seek the land. And who knows? Maybe they will. Maybe it's only a matter of time for *The Mermaid Translation* to arise and wash ashore.

1/27/11

Mailed a copy of *TMT* to Tom Robbins.

1/27/11

Sold 3 books to the Robert who told me about the elephant who lived in Whatcom Creek. His great-grandfather (another Robert) would listen to the Morse code operator tapping away at the train station. When he heard that the circus train was on the way, he would tell his daughter and she'd be the first to crowd the track to see the train pull in, thick black smoke, clowns and animals waving from the cars.

1/28/11

Sent an email to the student Underground Coffee House, hoping to do a reading of *TMT* there.

2/1/11

Standing here on the shoulder of the road in a familiar landscape, green hills marked by stone fences and hedges, some crows making for a big oak tree. I've been thinking about readings: I've had a terrible time with bookstores and venues either requiring fees, saying no, or just not answering me. I suppose at this stage the book is on its own, carrying itself, and traveling by word of mouth. I hear a muttering, a distant motor approaching on the road. I edge further into the weeds and watch. A little maroon colored open car rounds into view. It looks like a rowboat with wheels. The driver cuts the engine and coasts to where I am. Its tires rub into the flowers grown next to me. Even with his helmet and goggles on, there's something familiar about the driver. When he looks to follow the birds, I remember that black and white photo. It's J.D Salinger, the author who lived in the shadows. As he points out the empty seat in the sidecar, I decide why not? Maybe he's right. Who needs the hassle and gaggle of rejections and disappointments? All we need is to keep going. Which reminds me—there's a new book I'm writing—that's what I need to be doing.

2/1/11

Note from my publisher. (I'm thankful for all his work on this!):

"5 copies sent out today to orders...*Mermaids* going to Niagara Falls and Reno..."

2/10/11

Yesterday and this morning on the way to the bus stop, I heard a red wing blackbird calling from the iced-over swamp. Two more libraries have added *The Mermaid Translation* to their collections. Thank you to University of Colorado & Columbia University!

2/14/11

Bowdoin College library adds *T.M.T* to their Special Collections.

2/18/11

John Hopkins University has a *Mermaid Translation* in their library now.

2/21/11

2 more libraries add *T.M.T* to their collections. Stanford University & University of Iowa. I am very thankful. Also, this might be a good place for this journal to end, with *The Mermaid Translation* steaming off to the horizon like the bandstand in that old Marx Brothers film *At the Circus*, fading with music and a dot of light.

2/25/11

One submission was rejected this week, but today a story was accepted!

3/8/11

Bellingham Public Library has ordered 2 copies of book. Wonder if they will notice their part in the book (burning old telephone books during winter). Also University of Michigan has a book.

3/10/11

I was asked by a librarian here at work if I'd like to do a reading of the book in April here at the library. Of course!

3/14/11

Sent off a 3 poem submission and also another poem submission. Fingers crossed "Noah Road," "Lighthouse," "Unpolished" & "The Hula Hoop Hero."

3/14/11

Note from my publisher:

"Hey, I sold two *Mermaid Translations* in Kentucky...both to younger readers, college students."

3/15/11

Submitted 2 poems. "Good Luck Deer" and "The Seagull of 32nd Street."

OHIO SILVER MINE

On Easter morning, I bought tickets to fly to Ohio for the release of our new book *Selected Correspondence of Kenneth Patchen*. I can't get it into stores in my hometown, but Ohio is rolling out the red carpet.

4/25/12
Rain on the windshield
seagulls combing the air
over the parking lot

The airport shuttle bus only makes it as far as Burlington, about a half hour down the road then stops at the local station on a gravel lot near a Taqueria. The driver explains that our windshield wipers won't work. He goes inside the office, a little wooden trailer for awhile. Carl Reiner and Mel Brooks are in my headphones. When the bus driver comes back to us he explains there's another bus but they can't find the keys for it. This is a comedy. Meanwhile, the sky is clearing to a silver polish. He tells us he's willing to risk the highway without wipers and hopes the rain doesn't come back again.

The bus stops at the Tulalip Casino and a couple people escape off into the night. The driver is nervous about going further south. At Everett, we get off the road then back on. I see the sights repeating. We're going north. We return to the Tulalip Casino where we prowl into the long parking lot and stop beside an older silver bus with Las Vegas displayed on the destination sign. This is our new bus. In the black boggy puddles beside us there's the sound of frogs.

The day began this way earlier. I guess the tone was set when I left work to go to the dentist. I was having my temporary crown removed and a new one put on. They gave me the shots and prised off my crown and then they discovered the new one didn't fit. So with a numb mouth and my old crown put back on, I left for Ohio.

We finally made it to the airport at 10:15 P.M. After a long wait getting x-rayed and examined, if I hadn't been running I wouldn't have made it to the closing doors of the gate. I was the last person to board. The stewardess shrieked at me, "Scan your pass!" The flight was rough. A rocket to Ohio. 37,000 feet, 600 mph, it was -70 degrees outside, but I couldn't get comfortable.

Those little towns
flying over North Dakota
they mirror the stars
we fly the space in between

4/26/12
We made it to Detroit
just before sunlight.

Sleep that rushes in and hurries out
wakes me up with a start and
only a moment has passed.
Oh, but in that gone second
I was on a bed soft as a cloud.

I have four hours to wait
before the next plane leaves
to Akron. Watching people.

    On the flight to Ohio, I sit next to a man who thought I was going to a seminary when he spotted my Thelonious Monk book. From then on he talked the whole flight. He's going to visit his grandchildren. After all these years, he wants to enjoy life and live simply. He's been overseas, been to China for the sale of his company. He regrets that now—all the hours he spent working, chasing money—it was all about money. Now he lives in a 200 square foot pre-fab with his second wife from Guam. He wants to fly back there with her. He showed me her photo, standing in front of the picket fence of their little house in Rhode Island. His family all thinks he's crazy, but they don't listen. They work 12 hour days. They can't understand what he's learned. He's not wasting time, he's finally happy now.

    Tired, I have to wait for my ride. Tried to wait inside, but outside looks better—there's a metal bench out there in the air. In here the TVs are on, talking about JFK again. I bought an unsweetened ice-tea from the fountain and took it outdoors. White sky, thick clouds, breezy and cold, an Ohio flag clanging against the pole.

Two ladies get out of a car. They coo and say goodbye to the driver who pulls away with a toothpick in his mouth. A moment later one of the ladies runs back stops at the curb and waves at the disappearing car. "He's got my purse in the backseat…" she tells me. "I ain't going nowhere without it."

When Larry Smith shows up we drive the long road back to the house in Huron. Lots of trucks, the corn fields grown low, it's a season in Ohio I haven't seen for a while. When we park at his house I get out and hear a cardinal.

Good to see Ann again too. We catch up on things and Larry and I run through our presentation. It seems good.

Napping off the jetlag
I fell asleep and woke up
in Ohio.

After supper, we drove to Cleveland. It's early. We cross Detroit Street and went to The Root for chai tea and coffee. Then back again to the Lakewood Public Library, downstairs to the big room filled with empty chairs.

4/27/12

The Kenneth Patchen talk went great. Over twenty people were there, including the son of Jasper Wood, an artist featured in our book. Everyone was kind and appreciative—how great to see people like the work. After the reading also met Vlad the poet and he gave me his most recent book of poems saying, "my best yet." It has a silver rocket on the cover. We drove back home and I watched the clouds and sky get dark and a white planet shine.

Walking the dog to see the lake, I didn't think it would be so cold here. Sunny though. The lilacs and dogwood are flowering. Lots of starlings making electronic effects and the sound of Lake Erie roaring, brown waves white curled and cold as winter.

At the Goodwill, I open the door for an old lady pushing a shopping cart filled with tall metal flower stalks.

Went to the drugstore to get a toothbrush, something I forgot to bring with me. The spiral notebooks I like are cheaper here in Ohio, only 89 cents. I buy a toothbrush for one dollar and a five cent coin.

All this travel money, I have an envelope stuffed with twenties. It's nice to buy cups of tea and coffee, souvenirs, and not care what it costs…that is until I buy two silver charms that cost $20 each. Then I care.

I drive the Smith car to Oberlin. I like this countryside, the road going between farms. Mostly it's all winter colored. The Ohio green is still asleep. We park in town. The bookstore is an old Ben Franklin. There's a glass case holding the first City Lights Pocket Book for sale.

Every time I come here I feel the radio in me
turning on poetry. I want to write and write.
Is it just stepping out of the routine at home
and being away from the job mentality?
Or is it this place talking to me? Probably.
I hear the birds chirping and over in a yard
a lawnmower is going.

4/27/12 2:20 P.M.
The second time to the beach
the day has warmed up, the wind
died down, the water settled to glass
in the lake. The dog and I make our
footprints along the edge of land
and leave them to the wash.

Holding a baby
that warm weight
close to you

A big feast tonight: homemade spaghetti, salad and angel cake with strawberries. Four kids playing in a cardboard box, their voices go in and out of the house. Washing the dishes and stacking them clean. Once it got quiet again we watch a movie based on a story by Raymond Carver.

Knowing how hard it is to fly, I had to sort of struggle to get myself here. I told my friend Eric, "They want to pay me to fly out and talk about the new book. It's like being a real author," and he said, "You *are* a real author."

At night, a train goes by. It doesn't have that slow roll of a summer train, the clacking wheels that go on and on along the tracks with the long harmonica hello goodbye. This train is gone quick then it's quiet. No cricket sound yet, it's still too cold. They must be waiting underground or wherever with the rest of summer hiding.

4/28/12
A white sky, walking the little dog
a dove somewhere in the tree above
the calm neighborhood street
a vacant lot filled with the gray
round nodding heads of dandelion
survivors

Soccer fields
filled with people
swallows and
snow

Sure, there are family things I don't know anything about. We go our own ways. She lives in that place past a gas station on the corner where we turn. I have to control time when she shows, using a cane to walk.

Yesterday we drove through a town named Ceylon. Today we watched *Footprint of the Buddha,* set on the island of Ceylon. The film ends with the slow walk of a monk in the jungle, the birds singing him along.

Bumping along the white
edge of the clouds
the sun shining on the wing

God bless
the flying mother
caring for her child
she blows and soothes
and walks the aisle
calming down

Now it's done
back in Seattle
all the lights
like a tidepool

landing

The BICYCLE CHRONICLES

Today, Rustle got his old bicycle out of the barn and took off riding. We watch him circle the cul-de-sac easily and happily, his white t-shirt and blue jeans like some 1950s kid. There's no doubt the bike is too small though. Back at home I took a nap in the sun for a bit and then we got in the car.

We're on the way to a fruitless search at a used bicycle store. Samish Way is crowded with rush hour traffic. Just past the car wash, I see a woman point at the sky. I turn to look at what she sees…some crows up there are diving at a strange bird.

At first I thought it was an eagle, but it has a long wide tail like a prehistoric bird, an archaeopteryx, wheeling in the sky. I lose sight of it behind houses and trees. Winding down Holly Street, we go left onto State until we push against a wall of blackberry overlooking the dead place where the factory used to be. There are a lot of old buildings, sliding doors on rusted tracks and a bike trail that runs along the bay. There are also new buildings squashed in. They look plastic. On the other side of a locked silver gate Rustle points at a nice bike laid down like a zoo animal.

Soon we're at the bicycle shop. It's a jungle of parts. In fact it looks like the big leafy trees have grown them and dropped them everywhere. We enter an old garage and there are people, but they act like we aren't there. As if we are ghosts, we stand there and look around.

It resembles a World War 1 field hospital. Shadows and rust and darkness all the way to the back wall.

It's filled with dead and fossilized bicycles blown up everywhere, hanging from rafters bent and broken and freakish spray-painted experiments.

So we drift back outside to the yard. I'm right next to someone putting air in a tire. He doesn't notice us. He gets on and leaves. I wonder if it's something we've done. It may be every bad bicycle memory comes here to linger and yawn. We are the sound of ghosts as we hush out of there too.

The next morning on my bike ride to work it's still damp from the rain last night. I pass a garden, wet sea-grass, tips white with dots of pearly dew. I lock up outside the door and go inside to start all the computers and open the windows and begin the work day. I read an email note from the library director who tells us he won't be in on Fridays anymore so he can spend time with his son. I think about my two children who I only see when I get home, and five days out of seven I'm tired and is that how they think of me?

Finally I ride home and Rustle's little circus bike is asleep on its side in the front yard. Then I can see him down in the cul-de-sac riding something that catches the light. I gather our dog and we go there to look. He rides a new bike up to me to tell me the story. Today they went to Value Village and there it was! Only $7! It's a perfect fit and fast as a bird. He named it Indigo for the blue color paint and he rides in wide circles around and around until the first drops of returning rain.

The 5 YEAR OLD LAND

There are years
where they believe
anything you say
fairy tales
talking animals
everything is real

Growing older
that doesn't leave
it just goes
to another place

Suspended
on a thin line
pulled out far
to the clouds
like a balloon
you still hold to

WALKING with a FLOWER

Listening to you
I believe you too

Love is all
a heart as open
as a flower

Knowing
nothing else
matters

ONE RAINING NIGHT

One raining night, my daughter called
She was rehearsing a play at school
and her part called for her to wear
19th Century clothes and use an
English accent, awkward as a parasol.
I was the only one at home
left without a car so I went to the garage
and found other transportation.
Riding my bicycle took about five minutes
hissing wheels to get to her. I stopped
beside her and she hopped on back.
She told me about the shortcut
through the woods behind school.
Little did I know that when we left
the pavement, we seemed to leave
this century too.

The dirt path was unlit
I had to go slow and sense where
there might be holes or roots of trees.
She squeaked behind me and once
we dropped and slid off the path.
That's when I decided to stop
so we could walk instead.
The rain came and went
as it wanted to, the sky was a room
in a house with bad plumbing.
The rain puddles washed our feet
and the branches told us when

we were off course. She said
we were almost through the woods
to the paved road on the other side
when we heard the tiny sound of bells
like a village in the mountains
sheltered by hands of snow.

Someone was approaching us
using a staff with a lantern at the top.
The sound arrived with a glowing
green light that got so bright
we had to shield our eyes.
The air trembled with wings
you could feel them on your skin
as he led all those moths past us
along the path and into the night.

mist between the peaks

11/6/12
2 am
bus stop

NORTH CASCADES

I have spent a lifetime
staring at mountains
and they have
kept me in view

whether I'm here
or miles away
it doesn't matter

they are
always there
to pin down
this table cloth
of travels

The POETRY PHENOMENON

It began with an invitation from J. Genius on Monday, May 14, 2012 to join him at the big poetry festival happening in the county south of here.

"Let's scheme of a way to do that poetry reading and soak up some poetic beauty next weekend." And later on, he repeated:

"Can you do the Saturday reading? We'd each read 2 or 3 poems. 10:45-12:00 in a brilliant old giant haunted mansion. I even have 2 poems, maybe a 3rd. Then maybe some time to frolic La Conner or see a poet? What say you?"

On Friday, when I said I would, he returned:

"Let's plan tomorrow, eh? Are you bringing the family or flying solo? And what time would you like to meet? The open mic thing is at 10:45 so we should get there no later than 10:30—but I'm up for meeting at any time you feel ready—we could meet for biscuits and gravy at the diner in Mount Vernon at 9. What are you thinking, logistician?"

So I agreed:

"Yeah the diner at 9! I'll bring my *Northern Exposure* script and we can practice."

J. Genius:

"Excellent. I'll start practicing my Maurice Minnifield-isms. That guy was pitch-perfect. Of course, I had him in class…If the class were marooned on an island, he'd be the first to secretly bring up the topic of cannibalism with me."

Me:
"Can you give me the directions to that diner again? Exits and whatnot coming south on I-5. I think I remember but I could also end up like Amelia Earhart."

J. Genius:
"Right-o. Take the Kincaid Street exit, and turn right at the end of the off ramp. Go straight for three blocks (I think there are two sets of traffic lights) and take a right on 1st street (it's kind of screwy, because if you go right, it's 1st, but if you go left it's Cleveland). Then you just stay on First Street a few blocks until you see the good old Skagit Valley Co-op on your right—the Mount Vernon Cafe (the diner) is across the street from the Co-op—so it will be on your left. You can park in the Co-op parking lot, but there should be spaces around. Call in case you get Amelia'ed. I will be there in my derby and short pants at 8:57, grousing about like an expatriate."

That morning, I left Bellingham at 8:30, first stopping to get gas. I couldn't find anything good on the radio, even on AM where I hoped to find a 1950s oldies station. Finally I tuned to Spanish music just as I pulled off the highway. Driving down 1st Street, I happened upon J. Genius daydreaming along the sidewalk. I rolled down the window and bellowed,

"Hey Dummy!" startling him out of his thoughts. Once I parked and met up with him, he told me he was thinking of a poem. We went into the diner, found a booth and caught up for it's actually rare that I sit with friends and palaver. When it was time to move on to the poetry town, we took his truck through the farms.

Up on the hill, the ancient mansion loomed like a pair of wooden crooked praying hands gnarled together. We parked around the corner. There were clucks of people fluttering about on the tipped sidewalks. The houses all have gardens that lean out over. Up the creaking stairs, we entered the mansion. A waxwork woman at the desk in the doorway pointed our way to the reading room. But before it started, J. Genius took me upstairs to look for the ghost. We found a room with a spinning wheel and clouds painted on the ceiling. Outside, below, the town bent in the windows. J. Genius tried to trick me by starting a rocking chair and pointing out the ghost. There was a door with a Staff Only sign on it. A peek inside revealed boxes, shadows and sun motes and a mannequin draped in a sheet. Was that the ghost? It was 10:45, so we went back downstairs on those splintery steps and found our chairs.

J. Genius appraised the room and immediately said, "Everyone who's here is going to read." It was true. There was no audience, only fretting.

I read "The Shepherd from Iran" "Fox Subway" and "Bellingham Coal Train." I don't know who wants to hear them though. I guess they're for J. Genius and the ghost. The 1891 room creaked with heavy time. I watched the tapestry rug with its dramatic rendering of a leopard ripping into a deer. J. Genius read a ray of sunshine, a truck ride with his son and The Beatles on the radio. Because it was so uncomfortable in that old house, it reminded me of the castles I visited long ago, where you could feel the ghosts watching you. It wasn't hard to imagine a muse for every person, wandering the festival streets with them, some joyful and skipping or floating, others dragging along this mortal plane like some of the ones in this room. The reading ended when the podium crashed over and books flew. There really was a ghost! I was glad for the disruption, I needed the doorway outside. The street was very quiet. We were both wiped out. Across the channel I could see three shelters shaped like cedar hats on the Swinomish reservation shore. We needed to be near the water. "Is there any way of getting over there?" I asked. I followed J. Genius, stumbling the town, half thinking we'd run into Tom Robbins in his Spam t-shirt. He wasn't around. You can't even get to the water in this place, the dock has a No Trespassing sign. In not too long, we found the little white pickup truck, got in and crossed the red rainbow bridge to the other side. Past the cemetery with fresh cared for flowered graves, we parked in the asphalt lot. We went under the wide rim hat of the closest shelter and there were some plastic chairs. Maybe, we thought, we could borrow a couple and set them out on the sand? But all the chairs had been broken. So we walked to the beach and found a log to sit on. A crow watched us, made a sound then was gone. What is it about poetry readings? We couldn't figure it out. (Still thinking about it later, here's my idea: poems are a sort of spell, and when you use poetry for pain, like those flowers of Baudelaire, that's what appears.) I wished I had read my haunted short story "Bucket Head" instead. I even brought it along just in case. Oh well. After a while, sitting on the log watching the riverlike flow, we felt better and it was time to go. Leaving Swinomish, a yellow dog tied by a rope, Jughead's Fire Works, old trucks and boats buried in vines, a totem pole on top the hill.

It was fun to drive around the farmland outside of town. The tulips have dropped their petals, there's a purple crop of iris still, but I like the big farm trees, the poplars and those wide old rhododendrons. J. Genius pulled into a narrow road that took us to a field he wants to buy. It's all filled in with tall green weeds. He wants to sell his house and move here and I can't blame him. There's Mount Baker and all the hills of Skagit Valley. We crawled over the barbed wire fence and waded through the grass. There's even a pond. It's got a silver metal bridge connected to a rocky island. Taking steps out on it, a big frog hopped off into the thick water. J. Genius wants to plant a stand of Douglas fir and cedar, have his house facing south for the sunlight. It's a good dream, a big open field and you can just picture the vast array of stars turning on at night.

While he drove me back to Mount Vernon where my car was waiting, he told me a joke about a man who ate a lot of dogfood. I sort of did a terrible thing and ruined the punchline. Actually, his punchline was ruder than what I predicted. We got out and strolled over to the bookstore. There was nobody else in the place, we were all alone. Somehow we were drawn, ending up at the back wall, looking at the poetry shelf. We both agreed those old Laurel pocket editions are great, but honestly by now I'm a bit poetry'ed out.

IMAGINARY SOMEONE
writing by Allen Frost

Allen, you are meant to lead the life of a novelist-poet and eye want to help you

—TFK!, 1990

not to worry

Not to Worry, poetry collection, 2011
illustrated by Rustle Frost

ALLEN FROST DISCOGRAPHY:

Novels:

Blue Anthem Wailing (1986-87)
When You Smile You Let In Light (1988-89)
Bagdad Butterfly of Panama (1989)
Waterstories (1989)
Stars Become Sand When They Land (1990)
The Last Frankenstein (1991)
Sitting On A Bomb (1991)
An Entourage Of Travels And Circus Side-Show Attractions (1992)
Where They're Going And How They Live (1993)
I Can Only Imagine (1993)
A Big Book Of Yellow Paint (1993)
Keep Up Your Spirits (1994)
The Sun Does Shine (1994)
White Russia (1995)
Rome Used To Be The World (1995)
Fly Above It All (1996)
Paper Guide (1997)
Heaven Antenna (1998)
Crayon Fable (1998)
Harmonium (1998)
Jupiter Hill (2000)
Jackson Ferocious (2000)
Across The Street From The Holy Saint (2000)
Harmonica (2001-2002)
Velocipede (2002)
Lemonade (2003)

Coral and The Admiral (2003-2009/2018)
Rose Petal Lantern (2004)
The Next President (2004/2005)
Copper Kettle (2005)
White Pond (2008)
Sun Mountain Grocery (2009)
The Mermaid Translation (2006-2010)
The Schubert Story (2010)
Convenience (2011)
The Moss Temple (2013)
Roosevelt (2014)
Kennedy (2015)
The Orphanage of Abandoned Teenagers (2016)
Pinocchio in America (2015-16)
Homeless Sutra (2016)
Mountain Temple (2017)
Instant Crow (2017)
Simple Minded Sunshine (2017)
The Robotic Age (2017)
The Lake Walker (2017)
Walt Amherst is Awake (2018)
Fable (2018)
Island Air (2018-2019)

Poetry and Short Story Collections:

Bowl of Water (2004)
Another Life (2007)
Home Recordings (2009)
The Wonderful Stupid Man (2012)
Playground (2014)
Town in a Cloud (2011-12, 2014)
The Sylvan Moore Show (2015)
Lake Erie Submarine (2015)
A Hundred Dreams Ago (2017)
Almost Animals (2018)
Florida (2019)
The Welfare Office (2019)

Essays:

Elbows & Knees (2003-2013)

Fictional Memoir:

Imaginary Someone (2020)

Film Into Novel Adaptation:

Translation of Marcel Carné's 1937 movie *Drôle de Drame* (*Bizarre, Bizarre*) into:
Bees Are Everywhere (2002)

Super-8 Film:

Caruso (1995)
Screenplay and star; with Michael Paulus directing

Sound Recording:

Planet Fishing (1992) Recorded by Dan Hanrahan
Moth on the Moon (1994) Recorded by Rob Millis

Magazines:

4 Q (1988)
Cow (1990)
Pie In The Sky (1992-1994)
Mars Cheese Castle (1992)
Up (1994-1995)
Wave (1997-1998)
Such & Such (2008)

Self-Published Poem/Story Collections:

Elvis 42 (1989)
Lawn Veterans (1989)
The Creation Of The World (1990)
Poems In Zoos (1990)
The Shrinkers (1990)
Paying For Water (1990)
Water Everywhere (1990)
Good Deed Rain (1991)
Flora Rabinovitch (1991)
Fish Bicycle (1991)
Tree Frog (1991)
Sea Cow (1991)
Waterhouse (1991)
Food Bank (1992)
Burt Ives In Televisions All Over The World (1994)
The Jimbaroo (1997)
The End of Beryllium (1997)
Your Favorite World (1998)
Brand New Ghost (1998-1999)
Universal Thirteen (1999)
The Other Laugh (1999)
Royalty Toy Company (1999)
Little Italy (2000)
King Leopold's Slow Leak (2000)
Motor Car Dealer Will Travel By Balloon (2002)
One Eye Open (2002)
The 500 Pound Halo (2002)
Silent Machines In 9 Sizes (2002)
A Paper Cup (2002)

Fly With Umbrella (2003)
Trelawny Cable Car (2003)
Morning Glories (2003)
The Last Ohio Morning (2004)
The New Book Of Endangered Birds (2004)
A Parent's Guide To Raising Piranha (2005)
In The Summer Air (2005)
Sacred Heart Junkyard (2006)
Sinking Celestial (2006)
With The Utmost Kindness And Calm (2006)
Water Ladder (2006)
The Charts Of The Sea (2006)
Clinton Street To Galveston (2007)
Gathering Up (2007: Compilation of *Up* magazines, written 1994-95)
Wave Collector (2007: compilation of *Wave* magazines, written 1997-1998)
Ohio Time (2007)
Cow Catcher (2008: compilation of *COW* magazines, written 1989-90)
Bird Taxi (2009)
Radio (2009)
A Reversed Cat (2010)
The Yellow Tree (2010)
Animals, Ghosts & Outer Space (2010)
Signals (2011)
Not to Worry (2011)
Air Travel (2011)
Life in the Rain (2012)
A Week of Rain (2012)
Ohio Silver Mine (2012)

14 Animals (2012)
Travel (2012)
33 Landmarks (2012)
The Peaceful Island (2012)

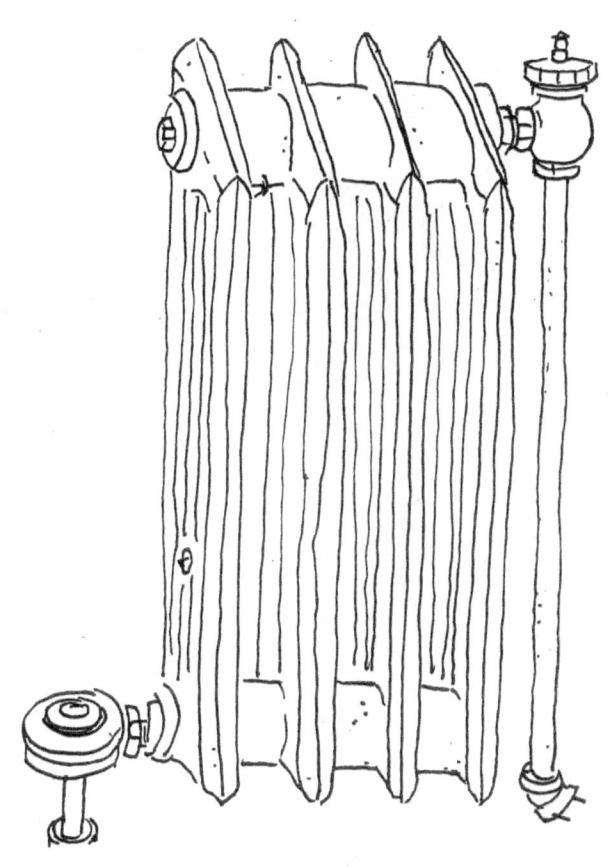

Illustration by Aaron Gunderson for cover of
A Hundred Dreams Ago, 2018

Books by Good Deed Rain

Saint Lemonade, Allen Frost, 2014. Two novels illustrated by the author in the manner of the old Big Little Books.

Playground, Allen Frost, 2014. Poems collected from seven years of chapbooks.

Roosevelt, Allen Frost, 2015. A Pacific Northwest novel set in July, 1942, when a boy and a girl search for a missing elephant. Illustrated throughout by Fred Sodt.

5 Novels, Allen Frost, 2015. Novels written over five years, featuring circus giants, clockwork animals, detectives and time travelers.

The Sylvan Moore Show, Allen Frost, 2015. A short story omnibus of 193 stories written over 30 years.

Town in a Cloud, Allen Frost, 2015. A 3-part book of poetry, written during the Bellingham rainy seasons of fall, winter, and spring.

A Flutter of Birds Passing Through Heaven: A Tribute to Robert Sund. 2016. Edited by Allen Frost and Paul Piper. The story of a legendary Ish River poet & artist.

At the Edge of America, Allen Frost, 2016. Two novels in one book blend time travel in a mythical poetic America.

Lake Erie Submarine, Allen Frost, 2016. A two week vacation in Ohio inspired these poems, illustrated by the author.

and Light, Paul Piper, 2016. Poetry written over three years. Illustrated with watercolors by Penny Piper.

The Book of Ticks, Allen Frost, 2017. A giant collection of 8 mysterious adventures featuring Phil Ticks. Illustrated throughout by Aaron Gunderson.

I Can Only Imagine, Allen Frost, 2017. Five adventures of love and heartbreak dreamed in an imaginary world. Cover & color illustrations by Annabelle Barrett.

The Orphanage of Abandoned Teenagers, Allen Frost, 2017. A fictional guide for teens and their parents. Illustrated by the author.

In the Valley of Mystic Light: An Oral History of the Skagit Valley Arts Scene, 2017. Edited by Claire Swedberg & Rita Hupy.

Different Planet, Allen Frost, 2017. Four science fiction adventures: reincarnation, robots, talking animals, outer space and clones. Cover & illustrations by Laura Vasyutynska.

Go with the Flow: A Tribute to Clyde Sanborn. 2018. Edited by Allen Frost. The life and art of a timeless river poet.

Homeless Sutra, Allen Frost, 2018. Four stories: Sylvan Moore, a flying monk, a water salesman, and a guardian rabbit.

The Lake Walker, Allen Frost 2018. A little novel set in black and white like one of those old European movies about death and life.

A Hundred Dreams Ago, Allen Frost, 2018. A winter book of poetry and prose. Illustrated by Aaron Gunderson.

Almost Animals, Allen Frost, 2018. A collection of linked stories, thinking about what makes us animals.

The Robotic Age, Allen Frost, 2018. A vaudeville magician and his faithful robot track down ghosts. Illustrated throughout by Aaron Gunderson.

Kennedy, Allen Frost, 2018. This sequel to *Roosevelt* is a coming-of-age fable set during two weeks in 1962 in a mythical Kennedy-land. Illustrated throughout by Fred Sodt.

Fable, Allen Frost, 2018. There's something going on in this country and I can best relate it in fable: the parable of the rabbits, a bedtime story, and the diary of our trip to Ohio.

Elbows & Knees: Essays & Plays, Allen Frost, 2018. A thrilling collection of writing about some of my favorite subjects, from B-movies to Brautigan.

The Last Paper Stars, Allen Frost 2019. A trip back in time to the 20 year old mind of Frankenstein, and two other worlds of the future.

Walt Amherst is Awake, Allen Frost, 2019. The dreamlife of an office worker. Illustrated throughout by Aaron Gunderson.

When You Smile You Let in Light, Allen Frost, 2019. An atomic love story written by a 23 year old.

Pinocchio in America, Allen Frost, 2019. After 82 years buried underground, Pinocchio returns to life behind a car repair shop in America.

Taking Her Sides on Immortality, Robert Huff, 2019. The long awaited poetry colleciton from a local, nationally renowned master of words.

Florida, Allen Frost, 2019. Three days in Florida turned into a book of sunshine inspired stories.

Blue Anthem Wailing, Allen Frost, 2019. My first novel written in college is an apocalyptic, Old Testament race through American shadows while Amelia Earhart flies overhead.

The Welfare Office, Allen Frost, 2019. The animals go in and out of the office, leaving these stories as footprints.

Island Air, Allen Frost, 2019. A detective novel featuring haiku, a lost library book and streetsongs.

Imaginary Someone, Allen Frost, 2020. A fictional memoir featuring 45 years of inspirations and obstacles in the life of a writer.

www.ingramcontent.com/pod-product-compliance
Lightning Source LLC
Chambersburg PA
CBHW031109080526
44587CB00011B/899